PRIMERS

Drawing

the motive
force
of architecture

Drawing

the motive force of architecture

PETER COOK

WILEY

Published in Great Britain in 2008 by John Wiley & Sons Ltd

Copyright 2008   John Wiley & Sons Ltd, The Atrium, Southern Gate, Chichester,
                  West Sussex PO19 8SQ, England
                  Telephone +44 (0)1243 779777

Email (for orders and customer service enquiries): cs-books@wiley.co.uk

Visit our Home Page on www.wiley.com

Reprinted May 2010

Other Wiley Editorial Offices

John Wiley & Sons Inc., 111 River Street, Hoboken, NJ 07030, USA

Jossey-Bass, 989 Market Street, San Francisco, CA 94103-1741, USA

Wiley-VCH Verlag GmbH, Boschstr. 12, D-69469 Weinheim, Germany

John Wiley & Sons Australia Ltd, 42 McDougall Street, Milton, Queensland 4064, Australia

John Wiley & Sons (Asia) Pte Ltd, 2 Clementi Loop #02-01, Jin Xing Distripark, Singapore 129809

John Wiley & Sons Canada Ltd, 5353 Dundas Street West, Suite 400, Etobicoke, Ontario M9B 6H8, Canada

Wiley also publishes its books in a variety of electronic formats. Some content that appears in print may not be available in electronic books.

Executive Commissioning Editor: Helen Castle
Project Editor: Miriam Swift
Publishing Assistant: Calver Lezama

ISBN   978-0-470-03480-4 (hb)
         978-0-470-03481-1 (pb)

Design and cover design by aleatoria.com
Printed and bound by Conti Tipocolor, Italy

Photocredits

The author and the publisher gratefully acknowledge the people who gave their permission to reproduce material in the book. While every effort has been made to contact copyright holders for their permission to reprint material the publishers would be grateful to hear from any copyright holder who is not acknowledged here and will undertake to rectify any errors or omissions in future editions.

The cover image is a collage by Nicoleta Rodolaki, produced in Peter Cook's studio, incorporating images by Iakov Chernikov, Peter Cook, Marjan Colletti, Marcos Cruz, Friedrich St Florian, Tobias Klein, Samuel White and Lebbeus Woods.

p 11 © The Frank Lloyd Wright Fdn, ARS, NY and DACS, London; p 13 © Sverre Fehn; p 14 © Miroslav Šik; pp 15, 43 © Collection FRAC Centre, photograph François Lauginie; p 16 © Cosanti Foundation; p 17 © Judith Wachsmann; pp 18, 186 © Coop Himmelb(l)au; p 19 © ISOCHROM.com, Vienna; pp 20, 21, 50-3, 72, 90, 108-9, 123, 153, 165-6, 173-5, 200-1 © Peter Cook; pp 22, 24, 27, 57, 58, 65, 67(t); 68, 78, 84-5, 101, 162, 182 © 2007, The Museum of Modern Art/Scala, Florence; pp 25, 26, 37-40 © Bernard Tschumi; p 28 © Jones, Partners: Architecture; pp 31, 32, 141 © Michael Webb; p 33 © Laura Allen; p 34 © Eric Owen Moss Architects; pp 35, 67(b) © Fonds Cedric Price, Collection Centre Canadien d'Architecture/Canadian Centre for Architecture, Montréal; p 41 © Reproduced by kind permissions of Pollinger Limited and the Estate of JC Robinson. Copyright © the Estate of JC Robinson; p 42 © Friedrich St Florian; pp 45-7 © Collection FRAC Centre, Orléans, photographs Philippe Magnon; pp 49, 102-3, 144-5 © CJ Lim; p 56 © Archives of the Wiener Stadtwerke-Verkehrsbetriebe, Stadtbahn map No 860; pp 59-60 © Archive Günther Domenig; pp 61, 129 © Avery Architectural and Fine Arts Library, Columbia University; pp 62-3, 114 © Zaha Hadid; p 64 © M Charney; p 69 © Deutsche Kinemathek Museum für Film und Fernsehen; p 70(t) © bpk/unknown photographer; p 70(b) © bpk/ Kunstbibliothek, Staatliche Museen zu Berlin, photo Dietmar Katz; p 71 © FLC/ADAGP, Paris and DACS, London; p 75 © Takasaki Architects; p 76 © Morphosis; p 79 © Aldo Rossi; pp 80, 120, 140, 185 © State Schusev Museum of Architecture (MUAR); p 82 © Yuri Avvakumov, AGITARCH Studio; pp 83, 191 © Xefirotarch/Hernan Diaz Alonso; p 86 © SITE Environmental Design, Inc, aka SITE; pp 88-9, 157 © Christine Hawley; p 93 © Chevojon Frères, Paris; pp 94, 192 © KOL/MAC LLC; Susan Kolatan and William MadDonald, Architects; pp 96, 137 © Drawings courtesy of Neil M Denari Architects, Los Angeles; p 98 © Marjan Colletti; p 100 © Fonds James Stirling, Collection Centre Canadien d'Architecture/Canadian Centre for Architecture, Montréal; p 104 © Courtesy of Gehry Partners, LLP; p 105 © Austrian Frederick and Lillian Kiesler Foundation, Vienna; p 106 © Edward McIntosh; p 113 © Nannette Jackowsky and Ricardo de Ostos; pp 115, 161, 194 © Lebbeus Woods; p 116 © Peter L Wilson; pp 118-19 © Will Alsop; p 121 © Staatsgalerie Stuttgart; pp 124, 127, 130 © Courtesy of the Deutsches Architekturmuseum; p 128 © Takehiko Nagakura; p 133 © Luke Chandresinghe; p 134 © Samuel White; p 138 © Inbo Adviseurs Bouw Amersfoort, drawings by Inbo; p 142 © Bartlett UCL/Julia Von Rohr; p 146 © Fujitsuka Mitsumasa, Gallery MA; pp 147, 170-1 © Nat Chard; p 148 © Billy Choi; p 149 © Yukihiko Sugawara; p 150 © Studio Daniel Libeskind; pp 151, 197 © Mark West; p 155 © Walter Pichler; pp 158-9 © Marc Fornes, Vincent Nowak, Claudia Corcilius; p 164 © RIBA Library Drawings and Archives Collection; p 168 © Geraldine Booth; p 169 © Marcos Cruz; p 180 © Graeme Williamson; p 181 © 2003 by realities:united, Berlin/ArGe Kunsthaus & Pichlerwerked GmbH, Graz; p 183 © MKDC Derek Walker/Andrew Mahaddie; p 188 © Gerald Zugmann; p 180 © Marcos Novak; p 196 © Ute Klein; p 198 © Simon Haycock; p 199 © Nikolaus Parmasche

Dedication

TO YAEL AND ALEXANDER who keep me chirpy

Acknowledgements

I should like to thank Helen Castle, Executive Commissioning Editor, for her wise and steady advice, Caroline Ellerby, freelance editor, for her resource and tolerance over the long period during which this book has been folded in and out of my various activities. Miriam Swift, Project Editor, for her deftness and understanding and Karen Willcox, freelance designer, for her spirited designing and Nicoleta Rodolaki of CRAB Studio for setting the atmosphere on the cover of the book.

Contents

Introduction

Perhaps the ideal way in which an architect can approach the act of drawing is to be unaware that he is actually doing it at all. Is it not a spontaneous means of summarising immediate intention? A form of jotting-down. Of course, other antennae of the brain are less encumbered. Shouting, murmuring, kicking or the wandering of the mind are less impeded by the necessary use of an implement, such as a pencil. The many effects on our consciousness of such implements has led to ceaseless pondering, whether it involves the impact of a lead pencil or the use of a particular computer program. Here lie so many of the debates about drawings themselves especially in a civilisation that is obsessed by the process.

Another issue that we have to get out of the way is the question as to whether architects' drawings owe more to the demands of architecture or to an artistic inheritance where the particularisation of a building matters little. Into this come the issues of consciousness, state of mind and motive.

We know that the professional writer or journalist evolves towards habits of description and the ordering of information that parallel a written piece: the pre-edit, the trained mind and the articulation of key observations. We readily recognise and accept such symptoms.

So how do we deal with the undoubtable parallels in architecture? These easily cross beyond the thresholds of technique, preoccupation or style so that the priorities of an ideal emerge – to be described in drawn lines that may enjoy those priorities.

1
Drawing and Motive

Much of the most memorable or most definitive architecture comes forth at a moment when a set of ideas exists as a form of attack: a retort to another set of ideas. The pressure of rhetoric or 'drive' needing to find an outlet, needing to shout loudly, to insist, awaken, reveal. The action will vary according to the temperament of the author and the means may well be highly conscious of the means used by the imagined adversary, whether this is an architect of an opposite persuasion or a sluggish and indifferent public. A parody of drawn mannerisms, or deliberately chosen 'cool' in response to 'hot', or sparse in response to complex, closely paralleling the architecture itself or its cultural background. Thus the extraordinary clarity, fierceness and buildable rhetoric of the work that came out of the immediate post-Revolutionary Russia attacked on all fronts through composition, graphics, colour, film, music, material and, of course, the power of the accompanying verbal rhetoric. As such, it can be seen as a coherent piece.

By contrast, one only has to glance at the kinds of drawings that accompanied Frank Lloyd Wright's Broadacre City (1932–58) and the subsequent Living City (1958), with their implications of endless Midwestern plains and soft, crafted materials and gruffly polite Midwestern conversation and values. They sought a natural expression of this through the medium of the deftly stroked coloured pencil: itself a fairly direct product of the soil.

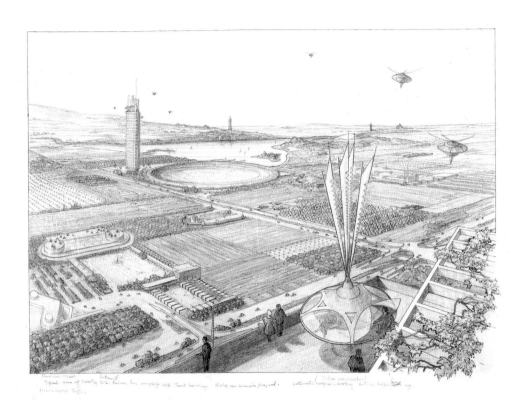

Frank Lloyd Wright, Living City, 1958. Aerial view: pencil and sepia on tracing paper, 89.5 x 107.3 cm. The Frank Lloyd Wright Foundation, Scottsdale, Arizona.

Delving into crazed territory, we realise that human will is an extraordinary phenomenon. If the desire is strong enough, the attack will be made – ideally with the same integrity as the two scenarios just described. But otherwise using whatever resources come to hand.

There may not always be any particular correlation between the significance of a powerful architectural drawing and its inherent 'artistic' merit, if we regard that in the illustrative sense. Such a relation between the representative aspects of illustration and selectivity will return as a central paradox in one's discussion. This questions the tradition that if a child displayed a talent for drawing and a grasp of mathematics, he or she would 'make a good architect'.

Finding the Appropriate Visual Register

The vexed issue of comprehension converting itself into reproduction will crop up throughout this survey, but for the moment one is relating only to the issue of motive. Herein lie thousands of moments of irritation and frustration on the part of (even) the motivated: when the concept – or maybe the image – of a project is sitting there inside one's brain, but the drawn version is but a poor thing. Inhibited by technique, inhibited by clumsiness or inhibited because the imagined notion has no real precedent in familiar imagery.

In parallel with the motive lies the link between a statemental notion and the assumed appropriateness of a visual accompaniment: another vexed territory that is perhaps the more so while we remain in a period in which philosophical and political motivation have the high intellectual ground for architectural commentators. It can be argued that during periods in which all drawn imagery, even the most visionary, was expected to refer to built or crafted form, the statement would gain power through the likelihood of the drawn image. Now it is likely that the spoken or written statement will have the acknowledged power and the drawing will be consigned to a supportive role. Could it be that this state of affairs has generated a subconscious will, on the part of the drawing makers, to run to more and more exotic forms, more and more provocative juxtapositions, in order to draw our attention?

Standing back from such complexities, we can admire the gentle power of the Norwegian architect Sverre Fehn's sketches. To have heard him as a lecturer or critic gives clues to their succinctness. His buildings are characterised by a talent for placement that is both deft and subtle, anticipating the grasping and channelling of light. They are dependent upon a clarity of intention that is carried by the single-move drawings.

The city library for Trondheim in Norway was to be, simply, an opened book. It was to be a large space inhabited by some internal bridge-like structures. The drawing made in 1977 for this unrealised project is a summary of the siting: the relation to the downtown immediately behind, the river and its riverside park. All carried in a one-minute jotting.

The relative agitation of the Museum of History at Ulefoss (1995) is probably a smaller, even faster drawing, its more scribble-like dynamic suggesting that Fehn was here making a determined point about the channelling of light and

Sverre Fehn, Trondheim City
Library, Norway, 1977.

Sverre Fehn, Museum of History,
Ulefoss, Norway, 1995.

the folding of structure. As a teacher, Fehn often had a pad of paper ready on
an easel and, to make a point, would run a simple linear profile or two across
it. Intriguingly, despite an acute sense of materiality and detail, he has refused
to waste time on elaborating these issues outside the working drawings.

Tectonics hardly seem to be the issue for Suburb of Tolbiac (1989) by
Czech-born Swiss architect Miroslav Šik. The implicit cynicism or critique set
up by the work is carried through the relative eccentricity of the chimneys
and roofs, which are, after all, traditional elements. Furthermore, it is
unequivocally at odds with any other Parisian suburb with its tight urban
streams of buildings that are nonetheless reminiscent of the tradition of
the cottage. The choice of colour and tone is not quite monochrome, nor
pastel (that, after all, would be far too sweet), but uses enough brownish-
black to create a brooding, angry atmosphere. Šik's mentor, Aldo Rossi,
rarely went this far, his drawings being more reduced and concerned with
the fundamental disposition of windows and edges, and sometimes even
quite joyful.

Miroslav Šik, Suburb of Tolbiac,
Paris, France , 1989. Colour pencil
and Jaxon pastels, 120 x 84 cm.

It is often worth noticing the parts of such a drawing that are not
particularly emphasised; such as the city seen in the background. A basic
light-side/dark-side indication on rectangular blocks says it all. The 20th-
century city, whether Paris, Central Park East or São Paulo, lies behind a
brooding woodland (or is it a fog?). The ultimate effect of the piece is to
imply a fierce arrogance that has not seemed to resonate outside a small
circle of admirers. In the late 1980s and early 1990s, the other members
of the circle of Analoge Architektur, based in Paris, Berlin, Stockholm and
Vienna, subscribed to the same palette and certain mannerisms, as did
their students.

It is, of course, easily possible for societal critique to be sustained by a
more positive mode of physicality than Šik's. In the 1960s, the Dutch
painter and Situationist Constant Nieuwenhuys sketched and formulated
endless pieces of invention – almost all of them lively. They sit interwoven
between the more proclamatory documents and graphics of his fellow
Situationist Guy Debord on the one side, and his own models on the other.
With those most seductive of all plexiglas platforms, webs of structure
and occasional domed folds, it is these three-dimensional icons that stay
in the memory as the accessible face of the Situationist International. So
the question to what extent the little drawings were always intended for
a supportive role, is intriguing. If one is already establishing the fact that

mere simplicity or apparent unhurriedness of a sketch is no indicator of its position in the creative path, one must argue that the spontaneity of the sketch or scribble is potentially far closer to the moment of 'idea' than the considered, laboured presentation piece. It is possible that in such a long and sustained piece of work as Nieuwenhuys' New Babylon (1956–74), the central motive was already established before most of the little drawings were made, yet they still carry in them a certain creative value: a 'quality of thrust' as it were. A dance to the theme of invention perhaps?

A vision that sustains more than half a lifetime and that even begins to be realised after many years may call upon the drawn evocation simply as the fastest way of suggesting the might and complexity of the thing. It is hardly the spearhead of the Arcosanti project, a city in the Arizonan desert, designed by Italian-born Paolo Soleri. After all, he has been a potter, a bell-maker and an architect. The power of Soleri's objects lies in the spatiality of his vessels: of every scale. He gathers younger creative people around him; he is happiest when forming pieces. Yet the Arcosanti proposition is an ambitious, hierarchical complex. In the 1970s Soleri would inspire architectural audiences of several hundred with the power of this great city that he would make. Drawings would suggest its might and, most

Constant Nieuwenhuys, New Babylon, 1963. Hardback book in a blue cloth-covered, slip case, H 41.5 x W 39 x P2.3 cm. Collection FRAC Centre, Orléans.

Paolo Soleri, Arcosanti, 1969. Black ink on paper, 27.9 x 41.9 cm.

importantly, show its vessel-like quality. A certain type of drawing was necessary: not crude, yet essentially thick and powerful in order to carry the vessel. To many, these have remained the vision of that city, and the particle of it that has been built has the validity of actuality: the guy made it! Yet the total ambition is a greater dream and many who appreciate the dream never make the journey to Arizona.

Experiment and Graphic Vision

At this point we must face a nagging suspicion: that the drawing can possibly be better than the reality. This clearly does not escape the world of commercial architecture where the cost of perspectives, 'renditions' and now – more often – fly-through movies can rival that to be spent on the actual design of the thing. In the case of Arcosanti, the drawings of the whole city were essential for the creation of the direction or thrust of the project and in the setting up of a surrounding euphoria – instances intrinsic to its initiation.

From the 1950s, the western American desert became a dream territory for another European architect, the German-Jewish émigré Konrad Wachsmann. Also initially a craftsman, Wachsmann envisioned giant hangar structures lying suspended over the seemingly endless territory. Yet as an adjunct to his more easily constructible propositions was his constant search for the 'universal joint' and a belief in the potential of structural fluidity. Anticipating the animated analysis that is now familiar to us, his twisted space structure has a shocking power. Its sinewy totality has become a key icon to the believers in a technological architecture who also resonate to its inherent lyricism.

Technically, it must have required painstaking concentration: of the tradition of Gothic tracery as much as of 20th-century positivism. It pointed the way towards the late 20th- and early 21st-century's fascination with linear plasticity and the morphing of material. It may be relevant that Wachsmann was a close friend of Albert Einstein. It may be equally relevant that he started his career learning joinery.

Konrad Wachsmann and students, Vinegrape, 1954. Drawing, 12.8 x 22.5 cm.

Vienna-based Coop Himmelb(l)au has successfully made an almost seamless transition from crazy experimentalists through an incremental series of built projects – few of which fail to intrigue us – and then to the making of large

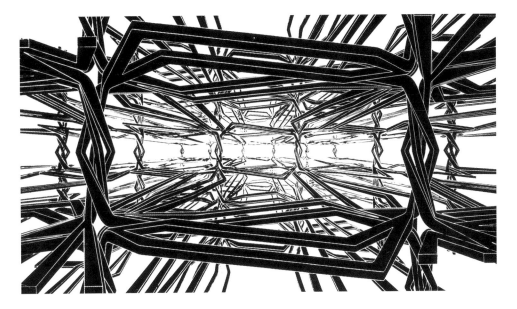

and complex buildings of great beauty. The sketches that have accompanied the work throughout come directly from two of its founders, Wolf Prix and Helmut Swiczinsky. On close examination, many of these sketches bear an uncanny closeness to the built object. In particular this applies to the work of the 'middle period' of the late 1980s and early 1990s in which a series of jagged spars thrust out in several directions. It is the surefootedness of these drawings that intrigues one, along with their sheer power.

Wolf Prix has admitted that as the fifth generation of architect-craftsmen he wandered around his father's studio from the age of six, respecting the elder Prix's ability to draw any detail precisely to size without measuring. One can reconstruct the progress from then on an artisan tradition of delineation that suits the Austrian precision with elements and the crafting of them. As the spokesman and the dynamo of the company, Prix has closely allied the mood of the rapier-like line, the stake in the flesh or ground (which we shall meet again in the work of Walter Pichler in Chapter 8), rhetorical battle cries such as 'architecture must burn', and the sheer élan that comes from the creation of extraordinary envelopes and extraordinary spaces.

Coop Himmelb(l)au, Open House, Malibu, California, US. Collage of a plan (on translucent paper) and a sketch (pencil on paper), 1983 and 1988–9.

Coop Himmelb(l)au, Busan
Cinema Complex/Pusan
International Film Festival,
Busan, South Korea, due for
completion 2011.

Models have always accompanied the work and now, of course, there are
computer renditions that even use showbiz techniques, such as the 2005
competition-winning design for the Busan Cinema Complex in South Korea.
From those classic Himmelb(l)au drawings remains a total understanding of
the enclosure and the measure.

My own procedure towards a sustained portmanteau project had nothing
of Prix's inherited reliability and my work has rarely strayed from a support
territory of mechanical line-guides and wobbly stencils, compasses and
constant measuring. The Plug-In City (1964) was a development out of two
earlier Archigram projects – the Nottingham Shopping Viaduct by Peter
Cook and David Greene (1962) and any competition-winning design for the
Montreal Tower (1963). It started as a series of small cocktail-stick models
that checked out the megastructure proposition, followed by the drawings of
the system of working parts. Only after these did I feel confident enough to
proceed with the key image: the axonometric view from above.

By this time, isometric and axonometric drawings had become a preferred mode of three-dimensionalisation (particularly in British circles – notably the axonometric projections of James Stirling's work that became referential images of the 1960s and 1970s), beloved by those of us who relied upon the apparatus of the drawing table and, in particular, the adjustable set-square. Yet you will notice that the drawing itself is maybe 65 per cent

Peter Cook, Plug-In City, 1964. Axonometric: cut-and-pasted printed papers with graphite and clear and coloured self-adhesive polymer sheets on grey paper-covered board with ink, 69.5 x 75.9 cm. Collection of Modern Art, New York.

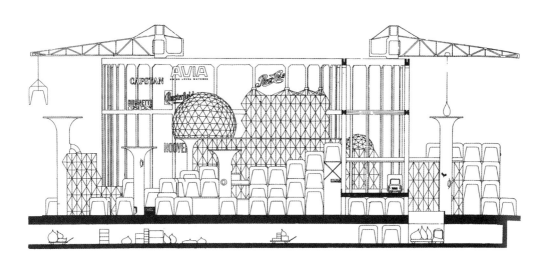

Peter Cook and David Greene,
Nottingham Shopping Viaduct
(precursor to Plug-In City),
UK, 1962. Ink line drawing,
25 x 15 cm.

freehand drawing. First, I made a plan on graph paper: this was essential for controlling such a complex piece and at the outset I realised that it would be an endless task if I were to draw every capsule from a stencil. Here I would have to risk my freehand abilities! There was another category that anyway needed to (symbolically) be more 'floppy', namely the inflatable covers to the public spaces with their (symbolic again) little air tubes feeding into them. By contrast the craneways and hovercraft track would need to be straight and determined: surely no place for freehand here.

The drawing was made in the evenings and at weekends, spanning many one- or two-hour sessions. Once under way, the thinking 90 per cent done, it became a steady task of moving across the drawing from one corner to the other: rather like painting the Golden Gate Bridge. From this description you will gather that such drawing is in no way spontaneous, but already a year or more into the thinking on the project and a season into its execution. Yet strategically, if the project was to be taken seriously (by myself, as much as by anyone else), it needed this total picture. Arguably, the long cross-section of the Plug-In City, Central Area, made a year later, has a wider range of architectural and systematic content, and the earlier, smaller section makes all the key decisions. Yet it is this aerial view that establishes the proposition – especially for non-architects. Its virtue is that it 'looks like something', and the City enters the history books.

Communicating with Clarity

This question of whether the motive of a vision, a project or a building needs to be recognisable is another ground for debate and possible confusion. After all, the Plug-In City (unless you were a specialist on the subject of European megastructure projects … and even then?) was hardly a familiar built form. Yet somehow, most viewers get the main idea from it, hopefully appreciating the subplot of the scheme that implies that of prefabrication can be romantic. Sverre Fehn could make his points with much less effort. Miroslav Šik could insinuate his points almost theatrically. To make mine, I needed an assemblage of parts.

From whatever starting point, it seems that clarity of priorities is at the centre of the issue. The need for illustration comes into play, even if it has to be conscious illustration for the sake of communication. Or in other words, the revelation of the motive may have to involve the architect in an intermediary distancing from its thrust in order to calculate the possible impact.

Here, I am still avoiding the territory of those bland 'visualisations' that rarely contribute much to the motivation of the work. As I move on to the discussion of the work of Arata Isozaki, Andrea Branzi, Bernard Tschumi, Cedric Price and Wes Jones, I remain in the territory of full and intense involvement on the part of these instigators – yet in every case, there is crystal clarity of communication to anyone with half an eye.

The collage will emerge within these pages as a critical tool of the 20th-century architect. Its continuation as a system of comprehension and as a creative trigger of lateral referencing, lateral thinking and morphed physicality

Arata Isozaki, Re-Ruined Hiroshima, Japan, 1968. Perspective: ink and gouache with cut-and-pasted gelatin silver print on gelatin silver print, 35.2 x 93.7 cm.

is assured by the advent of the computer. We can now so easily combine, mix, melt or otherwise encourage the hybridisation of ideas, tectonics, materials and images. Yet it is collage, in the sense of Braque, Picasso, Schwitters, which has caused the shockwaves within a hitherto stable world of conformity or homogeneity. We expected the countryside to flow gently from hedgerow to hedgerow, for culture and language (of form, as well as everything else) to develop steadily, for cities to absorb the new according to circumstantial requirements.

Thus Japanese architect Arata Isozaki's collage commentary on Hiroshima, Re-Ruined Hiroshima (1968), is multiply telling: it uses his own highly sophisticated sensibility to the full, with such a depth of knowledge of 20th-century art, culture and politics that he knows just how to confront us with the shock and tragedy of the situation. It is a piece of calculated rhetoric, yet at the same time containing such skill with the assembled parts that he can present his fragments of megastructure as both construct and symbol, both architecture and pictorial element, both collapsing and about to go forth. They pitch the mood as both negative and positive, though his own explanation is that of their being 'dead architecture'.

In many ways, Andrea Branzi's proposition of No-Stop City (1969), made when he was part of Italian supergroup Archizoom, is equally bleak. It exists as a critique of Modernist architecture and as a parody of the idea of a planned city. The drawing of the plan of its Residential Park is in itself a comment on a typical town-planning drawing. The biomorphic forms are placed somewhat haphazardly across a form of 'board game'. The green patches are parks, and the snakes of rectangular components are the housing. Yet at the same time the project has sufficient authenticity within it to be really challenging to other architects: the lift shafts really do look like lift shafts, complete with the counterweight drawn in, as in a working drawing, and the towers really do have a lift and a staircase drawn in correctly. A more sketchy version would not present the same challenge.

In equally haunting works, the challenge to conventional, pragmatic architectural thought is built up by the accumulation of information. A series of closely related and closely argued diagrams succeeds in Bernard Tschumi's Manhattan Transcripts (1979–80). They remain among the most telling architectural statements of the late 20th century. They have the task of bringing the viewer to the understanding that space and event could be generically at one.

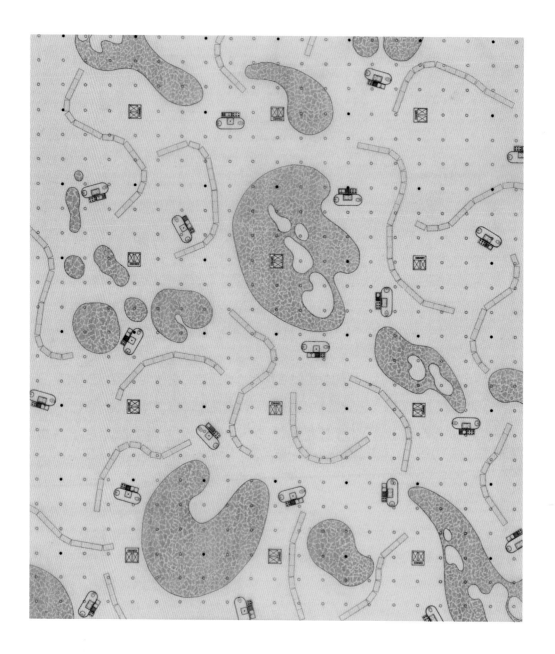

Andrea Branzi, Residential Park, No-Stop City, 1969. Plan: ink, cut self-adhesive polymer sheet, and pressure transferred printed film on tracing paper, taped to paper, 99.7 x 69.5 cm. Museum of Modern Art, New York.

Each point is made through a series of three square panels, where 'photographs direct the action, plans reveal the architectural manufacture, and diagrams indicate the movements of the main protagonists'. The narrative quality comes through the deliberately grainy photographs (Tschumi is a great follower of films), the 'plan' arrangements are sufficiently intricate (with road edges marked by a double line) and the abstractions (deliberately) recall choreographic diagrams used for the ballet. As an adjunct, Tschumi uses a series of tough stylised perspectives and axonometrics to move towards architectural propositions. They are not quite total propositions, since they are bulk form, with the occasional window, colonnade and even classical cornice usually juxtaposed in a shocking manner. Tschumi then uses a stark convention of black and two shades of grey that is enough to carry the formal and spatial story with some of the same level of abstraction as the grainy photographs. The Transcripts deal with an apocryphal narrative involving the Park, the Street, the Tower and the Block. There is a murder plot involving flight and collapse, there is an architectural motive involving the relationship between time and proximity, between collision and juxtaposition.

Bernard Tschumi, The Manhattan Transcripts, Part 4: The Block, 1979–80 (excerpts). Pen, ink and photographs on vellum, 45.7 x 76.2 cm.

We shall see in Chapter 2 that the Parc de la Villette that Tschumi built a few years later (1982–98) may be the playing-out of some of the method and certainly the formality of the Transcripts, but the ordering and the dynamic of those black-and-white squares remain in the mind as much as the Parc.

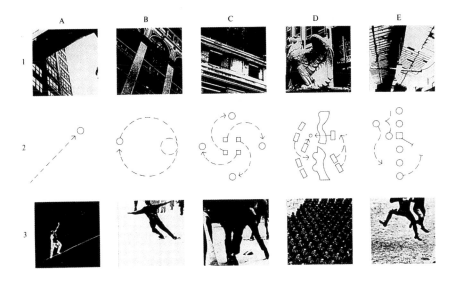

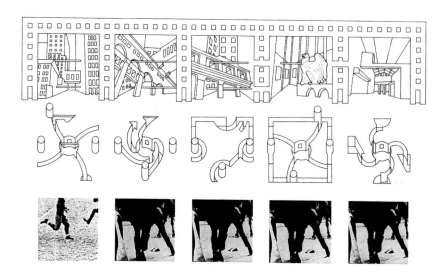

Bernard Tschumi, The Manhattan Transcripts, Part 4: The Block, 1979–80 (excerpts). Pen, ink and photographs on vellum, 45.7 x 76.2 cm.

If Tschumi produced the most disciplined and filmic work, Cedric Price can be described as the most fundamental thinker in the explosion of architecture that took place from the 1960s to the 1980s. Few of his works lack motive, few are just the playing-out of technique or infill information. Of the many that need to be discussed, I start here with a portmanteau image of his most discussed project: the Fun Palace (1959–61). We shall discover the poignancy and strength of smaller, sometimes 'commentary' pieces, but the general view of the Fun Palace project is powerful because it is readable at two levels. First, it is a straightforward picture of a large shed, with an understandable structure. Second, though, it reveals some slightly quirky conditions here and there, usually by way of Price's deft use of white patches and little hints – almost cartoon-like – of people doing funny things.

In fact it was a summary statement of a whole series of strategies and devices in which the elements of the building and its contained apparatus could be turned, folded, draped, bugged for sound – morphed, in fact, for constant change of programme or illusion. Dynamic being dragged back into architecture. The reassuringness of the general proposition becoming a giant stage into which the limitations of everyday life could be exploded.

If Tschumi brings to bear the disciplined French-educated mind together with the starkness of *cinéma-vérité*, Price distils out the jaunty, lovably ironic (in a quiet way) world of English artist-illustrators such a John Piper or

Osbert Lancaster. His drawing style is almost deliberately throwaway, but at the same time completely explicit. Tschumi came to England to escape the cloying French scene of the 1960s and Price was his early inspiration. That the mannerism of the work is so different, yet some of the fundamental philosophy so linked, raises an interesting question: whether or not the mannerism of a drawing can ever be definitively appropriate to a set of ideas?

Many groups of architects have suggested that it must be so. Especially the followers of a hero: take the example of Mies van der Rohe who established a clear and instantly recognisable way of planning buildings, a clear set of mannerisms and details. His innumerable followers could make precise, hard ink drawings that continued the atmosphere of the chosen architecture right through the process. Certain schools of architecture instil rules of procedures that are so dogmatically *de rigueur* that few students would dare to deviate, and those same people draw with the same mannerisms for the rest of their lives. Tschumi and Price evolve sets of mannerisms that are (once developed) simple to carry out and capable of adapting to a wide range of propositions, carried through in both cases from a clear motivation and combination of spirit and analytical clarity.

Cedric Price, Fun Palace for Joan Littlewood, Stratford East, London, UK, unbuilt project, 1959–61. Aerial perspective from cockpit: cut-and-pasted painted paper on gelatin silver print with gouache, 22.2 x 26.7 cm, date of drawing unknown. Museum of Modern Art, New York.

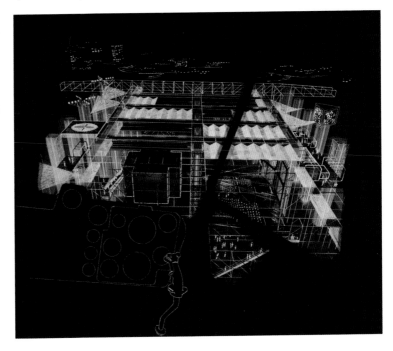

Propositional architecture dominates this survey because it carries with it the conscious wish to state a position, almost always distinct from the commonplace, the vernacular or that with which the public is familiar. The Meadow's Edge Cabin (1995) by Los Angeles-based architect Jones, Partners: Architecture exists to one side of this by virtue of its apparent straightforwardness, but then, like the detail parts of the Fun Palace, a second glance raises questions. As a collage it is careless in the placing (one might say the 'plonking') of the drawn house upon the photographed piece of woodland. As a building, however, its audacity dawns upon you: the components may well be almost droll in their ordinariness (stripped wood panels, straightforward windows, louvres, solar panels) – nothing here to disturb. The arrangement, though, is heroic, and this modest building actually contains a tower, a bridge and a separate pavilion.

Jones, Partners: Architecture's known interest in the mechanical and in components is harnessed to a conscious or subconscious confrontation. The timber returns to trees. The hut returns to the woods. 'Plonked', it can go anywhere. It is just a little ordinary house – but of course it is not. In a gentle manner, Jones, Partners: Architecture picks up some of Miroslav Šik's attack. The very matter-of-fact manner of the drawing is immensely important to the statement. Any attempt to make the imagery more subtle, any additional information, any wider palette of colours, would lose it.

Jones, Partners: Architecture, High Sierras Cabins, Meadow's Edge Cabin, California, U.S. 1995. View from west: digital drawing.

2

Drawing and Strategy

Watching a building under construction fascinates almost everybody, and following the design progress of a project before construction (often riddled with frustrations) is even more fascinating. Unbuilt projects can also contain several layers of development, intentionally or not, or consist of particular roles played out by particular drawings. In a few cases, a whole set of intentions can be summarised by a single drawing. Perhaps they spring from the comprehensiveness of medieval panels or ancient scrolls in which a whole series of interdependent events are separately located, but then to be read as part of a comprehensive strategy.

Maps are more intriguing since they must incorporate a whole range of criteria that happen to physically coincide – sometimes quite oddly. But then, real-life urbanisation contains a myriad of circumstances that somehow have to coexist. The poor old map has to try to either concentrate on one aspect such as the location and name of streets, or deal with the business of drawing out the significance of one system and the displacement of another. My earliest memory of such things was in my father's office at the end of the Second World War where the walls were covered in a variety of different maps: some with flags and pins, some with strings, some with patches. With him, I visited the sites of large mansions in the English Midlands where he would make or implement decisions to requisition them for use by the army. Thus at the age of six or seven I quickly began to make connections between the flags and lines and consequently started to invent maps myself.

On the walls of restaurants or the homes of ambitious neighbours were etchings of towns: 'A Prospect of Nottingham from the South-West' or such. The convention was to make sure that the castle and the churches were prominently visible among the endless scratchings of the etcher. Common houses and trees were (I suspect) filled in to a formula?

So imitating these became a complementary game to the map-making, though the essential difference took some years for me to recognise. If my route into architecture lay somewhere between the mansions, the pins and the etchings, perhaps I should have noticed the links and the differences. In a sense, I am now about to discuss certain architects who present the equivalent of the 'Prospect from the South-West' – a drawing that purports to show the whole conglomeration, but has hidden within itself some deliberate hierarchies and distortions. If the aim was to heroise the city, it comes pretty close to the intention of many architectural propositions.

The map, on the other hand, aided by abstraction and the necessary choice of a symbolic language, has the opportunity to insinuate a strategy. It relies more on the intelligence, the experience, and the interpretational skill of the map reader. It is open to scrutiny and plenty of misinterpretation can occur.

The Seen, the Unseen and the Seductive

Being inspired for many years by fellow Archigramer Michael Webb's Temple Island (1988) project and having heard him lecture on it several times, I am bewitched by the drawings themselves as much as by the narrative. By this time, Webb had already produced the definitive Furniture Manufacturers Association Headquarters (1957–8), Sin Centre (1962), Cushicle (1966) and Suitaloon (1967) (we shall meet some of these later). He developed a drawing style for each – as appropriate. Yet Temple Island meant more, for it not only exists as a major essay in observation, perception and geometry, but is located in his home town of Henley-on-Thames – the languid, gentile home of the Henley Regatta, an event that centres on rowing on the river. The movement of a boat along a straight stretch of that river is the key to his proposition regarding the spaces *behind* the trees. The tantalisation of the unseen. The constant reconfiguration of this unseen as you move forward. That this master of the extant physical object should choose to deal with the unseen was in itself exciting. That he should then wish to celebrate two special objects was admissible. The Temple on its island is a romantic nod towards an unavoidable link between the Romantic and the classical. By

Michael Webb, Temple Island,
Henley-on-Thames, Oxfordshire,
UK, 1988. Oil on prepared
illustration board, 65 x 65 cm.

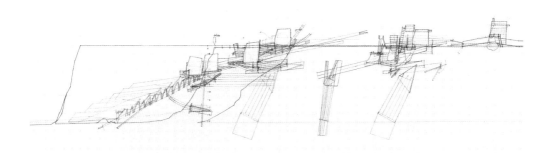

Mark Smout and Laura
Allen, Village for a Retreating
Landscape, Happisburgh,
Norfolk, UK, taken from the
Augmented Landscapes
projects, 2005. Paper and pencil.

contrast, the other celebrated object, the submarine, is the creation of the
geometrical hypothesis itself. The submariner must lie prone and observe
through a small porthole, having the perfect conditions for observing the
spatial denouement.

It is as if these three conditions – the map, the Romantic island and the
vehicle – must exist in extremis, while still being absolutely necessary to
each other.

In a similar way the Norfolk objects that the London-based architects Laura
Allen and Mark Smout lay out along strips of beach and flatlands in their
probings of urban and rural landscapes have a similar interdependency; as
illustrated here in Village for a Retreating Landscape (2005).

At first sight, the inclusion of Los Angeles architect Eric Owen Moss' Fun
House (1980) might seem to be odd at this point: very much an illustrative
piece, high in its visual coding and picturesque in the extreme. Yet look
a little closer. This is an early work and predates the plethora of formal
exploration that underwrites his more recent buildings in the regenerated
studio town of Culver City near LA. The Fun House clearly enjoys itself – all

Michael Webb, Temple Island,
Henley-on-Thames, Oxfordshire,
UK, 1988. Oil on prepared
illustration board, 140 x 98 cm.

Eric Owen Moss, Fun House, Hidden Valley, California, US, 1980. Collage, pencil and ink on Mylar.

along the line. The collage drawing here divides into a left-hand strip which is a fairly straightforward (if decorated) axonometric of the two semicircular 'pavilions', and a larger, right-hand conglomeration of surfaces, patches, bits, pieces, interferences plus some occasional nods in the direction of tectonics (but not too many).

The strategy is one of seduction: to establish a certain credibility that we are dealing with architecture and to then open up a Pandora's box of goodies. If the form of the house is not enough – come inside and really have fun!

The Pandora's box offered by Cedric Price in a project for a Pavilion in Perth, Australia (1983) emerges item by item, based on the dispersal of a wide range of components: screens, posts, trusses and rotating elements are the parts of a composition that never needs to be seen as a totality. It is much more to do with accumulation and action, and the appropriate devices for a certain moment in time. Similarly, the drawings and graph-paper patches themselves are deftly chosen fragments: a scrapbook almost, presented

Cedric Price, Pavilion in Perth, Australia, 1983. Plans, sections, elevations and details: reprographic copy, 14.7 x 20.9 cm.

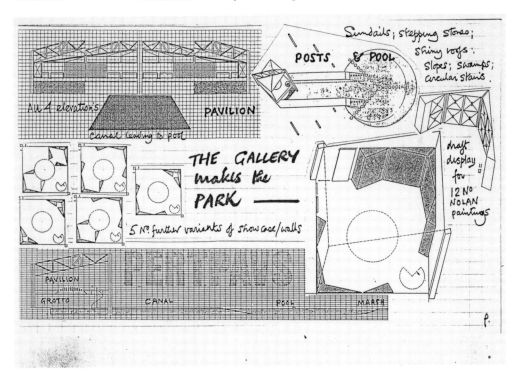

(deliberately?) as such. Price again uses his cartoon-like technique and straightforward handwriting. One is expected to review the whole page as it comes: as a series of equally important elements of a componented plan, with the architect spontaneously (and with considerable intelligence) thinking on his feet. The drawings are thus a totally unfiltered representation of this same directness.

The Strategy of Implementation vis-à-vis Confrontation

Returning, again in train with Cedric Price, we find Bernard Tschumi caught in a far more loaded situation. After all, the Parc de la Villette (1982–1998) was one of the *Grands Projets* for Paris. It was won against stiff competition, and a discrete strategy of implementation needed to be invoked if Tschumi himself were not to be left with the reputation of the overall concept and a few minor corners of building, but a myriad of strange buildings by others fleshing-out the concept.

A programme matrix of red, Neo-Constructivist pavilions had to be spelled out simultaneously in a degree of explicitness that made them seem both likeable and possible and at the same time consistent with the abstracted statement that they could be key to a marked and coded territory. The set of eight drawings described as *planches scénographies* constantly reiterate the grid of red squares, with a sequence of panels that explore the linkages, the geometries and the application of pavilion to path. They begin to play with the possible variants of pavilion (box) to antennae. On one drawing they jump down in scale to remind us of the total park.

Elsewhere they describe the armatures of paths crossing or glancing. The underlying dynamic running behind the mannerisms of the parts is clearly a development of the Manhattan Transcripts (1979–80) theme (see Chapter 1). Here, it has to be formalised into a series of pieces that talk across to each other through space, rather than collide. Here, the language of its description (just as with the language of its execution) has to be more publicly acceptable than stark black-and-white. The red preoccupation works graphically, linking the key elements, usefully connecting through the Constructivist language to the Revolution and its heroics – always underscored (in the matrix) by a grey 'shadow' or, in the three-dimensional elements, by shade or shadow. Thus it sits clearly, able to pass seamlessly between 'plan' and 'view', between map and prospect.

Bernard Tschumi, Parc de la Villette, Paris, France, 1982–98. Drawings created for the publication *La Case Vide*, Architectural Association (London), 1985.

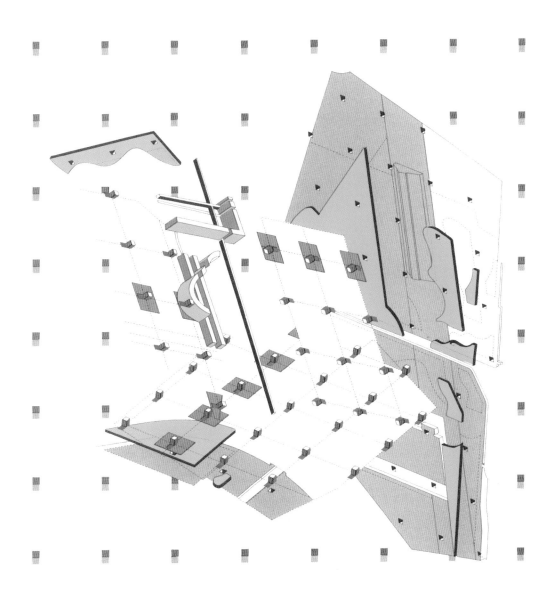

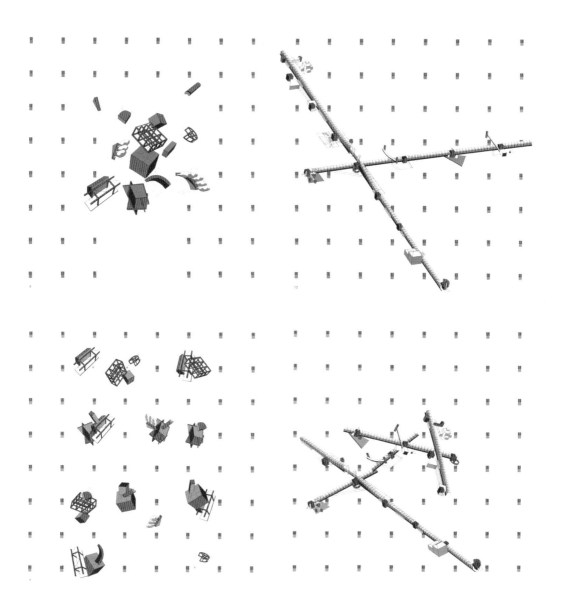

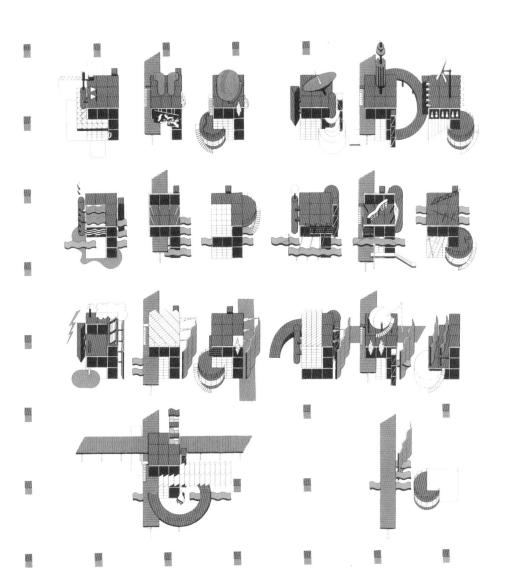

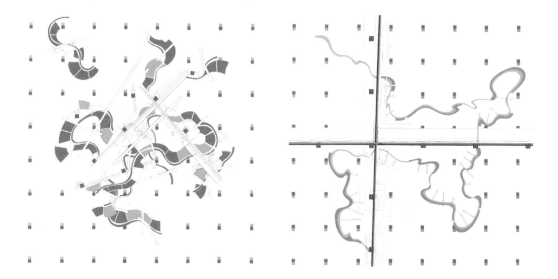

Moving on from Tschumi, who always retains an intellectual control over the situation through guile and wisdom, to William Heath Robinson – perpetrator of 'English Silly' – might seem absurd. Tschumi is bringing strategy, form and sophisticated reference to a general public out for the day. Heath Robinson chose to tweak that public with notions of the unlikely (but nearly possible) in a strategy of confrontation. This English cartoonist of the early 20th century remains a reference for all who subscribe to the spirit of invention. Not a little of the naughtiness that can be found in early English 'High Tech' comes from his propositions, which incorporate strings, pulleys, buckets, or the waggling of the big toe to set up a chain reaction.

That which is titled *Carrying out the Correspondence Course for Mountain Climbing in the Home* (1928) taunts us with a construct in which, just at the point of maximum absurdity, we notice that the cup of tea awaits the successful mountaineer. As with Price, it is essential to base the new or extreme proposition among the *very* ordinary.

The City Transfigured and the Soho Project

Alongside the ordinary, the strategic importance of the unseen is with us at every turn in an electronic culture. The Austrian-American architect Friedrich St Florian in the 1970s was one of the first to draw attention to this in his 'City' of the sky, depicted in his New York Bird Cage (1968), which effectively

William Heath Robinson, *Carrying out the Correspondence Course for Mountain Climbing in the Home*, 1928. Ink and watercolour on paper, 49.4 x 37.5 cm.

draws upon the significance of air traffic lanes in defining a comprehensible urban condition by way of control and procedure without (hopefully) events or elements between: just space. In certain respects one can read the project in two ways – both as a statement about the physical presence or non-presence, and as a statement about the strategy of intention.

At a similar period, St Florian was experimenting at MIT with lasers and, again, the 'instantly seen but not present' linear condition. In a sense, this work is as much about the strategy of drawing as if it existed on paper,

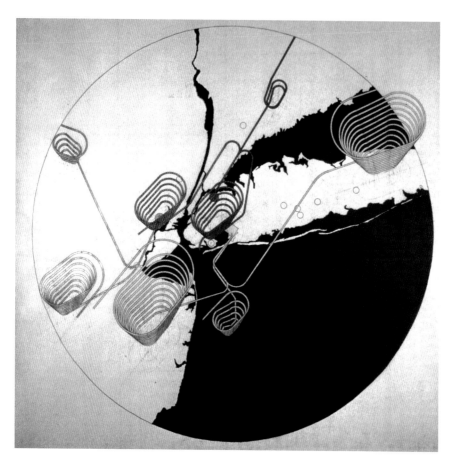

and thus raises the question: do we need paper (or any other markable field) in order to make a drawing? Is the act of drawing a gesture? Almost certainly. Could it exist without a certain moment of decision-making? Almost certainly not. Intriguingly, St Florian did not continue to pursue these lines of enquiry and it seems that others who have contemplated them have used them to support more elaborate projects. In this sense, the rapidity with which the computer has developed could be described as having inhibited the slow drip-drip of the possible absorption of notions such as that of the *conditional* presence of objects. The computer, though wild and wonderful, has treated us to more generations of delights to the eye that can also be fully rationalised and immediately related to the *tangible*. Too tempting for us to resist.

Friedrich St Florian, New York Bird Cage, 1968. Coloured pencil on sepia print, 85 x 89 cm. Museum of Modern Art, New York, Philip Johnson Fund.

Yona Friedman, Spatial City, 1959-60. Ink and collage on paper, 21 x 29.7 cm. Collection FRAC Centre, Orléans.

A transfigured city can stay in the mind because it can nearly exist – it can be related to the pre-existent city. It is by no means abstractly conceptual. It might, of course, be unlikely, but always possible. That one such city could exist not only in proximity to the old city (as my Plug-In City of 1964 was to do – see Chapter 1), but actually straddle Paris is shocking in its presumption. Somehow, the Hungarian-born French architect Yona Friedman was able to charm us into considering this proposition in his Spatial City project (1959–60). His abilities as both a cartoonist and a mathematician were harnessed but, as with Cedric Price, in a suitably deft manner. The megastructure sitting over the city contains some buildings, but their presence is somehow that of an encampment or at most a Mediterranean coastal resort with thin, tented awnings and delicate connections. In another drawing a crocodile has cheekily swum up the Seine and the project wonderfully avoids the over-explained heaviness of many northern European visions. At the same time it has remained for several decades as the prototypical megastructure, sustained by the most cartoon-like of the series, whereas the more architectural sections and elevations have receded back to the status of support diagrams.

The key strategic role of a strict series of six comparable diagrams was set in my mind even when I made the first general drawing of the airship version of Instant City (1968) and its physical model in 1969. The issue of gentle, almost nonchalant, appearance was central to this version. If the earlier, trucked version was about temporary transformation (where Marshall McLuhan and Andy Warhol could suggest momentary fame for a person, I could apply the same notion to a place), this was about technique.

The how, the when and why could be explained by dangled wires, lowered drapes and people running around or partying underneath. I have never been shy of using lettering: large if needs be. Inevitably I found myself using that lettering in a similar manner to the general aesthetic of the rest. I saw these not as architect's drawings, but as a desperate attempt to make sure that everybody knew what the thing was about. Closer to the instruction manual than to the 'Prospect from the South-West'.

Stranger and more winsome, Michael Webb's Suitaloon diagrams of 1967 (that we shall see in Chapter 7) have much the same intention. The accumulation of apparatus extends over many stages and the combination of the man and the woman in the story somehow maintain the logic of the mechanical augmentation while at the same time being quite

Peter Cook, Instant City, Airship Sequence of Effect on an English Town, 1968. Ink on tracing paper, 32.2 x 46 cm. Collection FRAC Centre, Orléans.

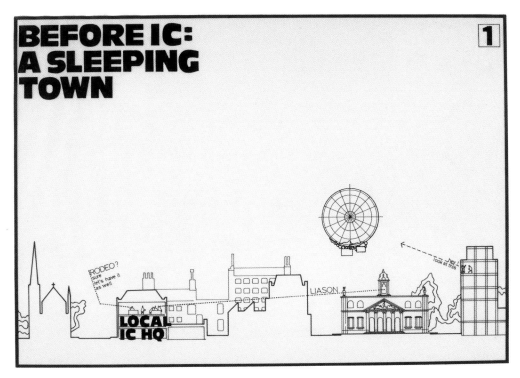

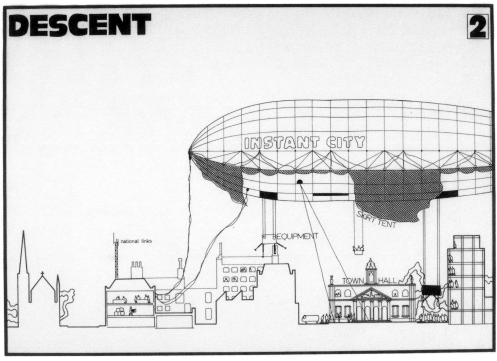

EVENT

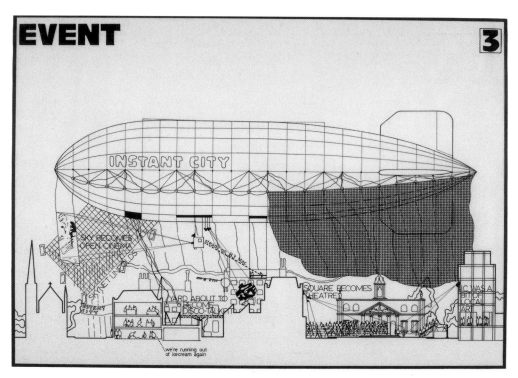

HIGHEST INTENSITY

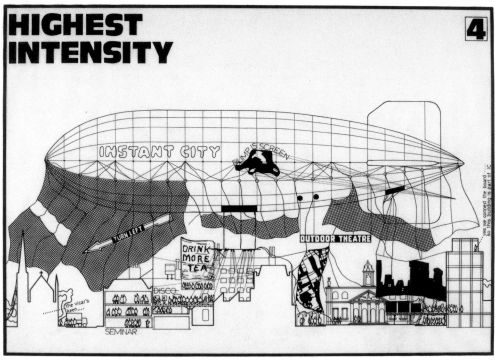

INFILTRATION

5

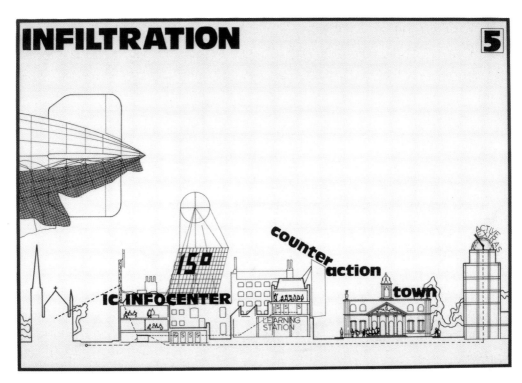

15° IC INFOCENTER · LEARNING STATION · counter action town · ACTIVE EXTRAS

NETWORK
TAKES OVER

6

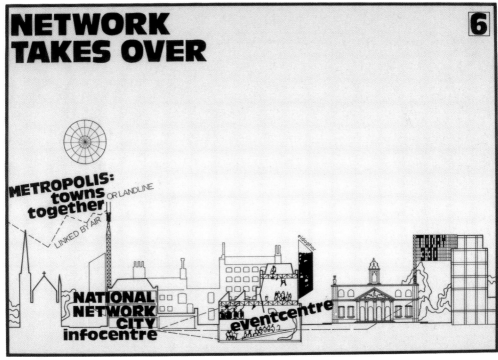

METROPOLIS: towns together · OR LANDLINE · LINKED BY AIR · NATIONAL NETWORK CITY infocentre · eventcentre · eidophor

sweetly romantic. The manner of the drawing can therefore remain quite straightforward.

It is possible that the increasing use of computer-generated sequences in which accumulation and transformation from one state to another will have sent such sequence sets into a byway of the world of communication. Yet we may well return to them for they are in many ways more essentially analytical than a more seamless, flowing sequence. Step-by-step, focused moment by focused moment, the strategy is played out.

The Malaysian-born, London-based architect CJ Lim's Soho project (1995) suggests strange will-o'-the-wisp occurrences that are made up of invented robotic figures that dart into the narrow alleys. They appear suddenly, they configure and reconfigure with great rapidity. They are not easily recognisable from any typical architectural, aeronautic or vehicular model. As a result, Lim has three major tasks in their description: to track the sequence, to track the change in the physiognomy of the pieces, and to track the way in which they insinuate themselves into these very localised places – and then dart away again.

The Advanced Five-Finger Exercise and Fast Company

This is a kinetic event, yet intriguingly traceable through the series of small sketches and diagrams. The interdependency of the three conditions gives a spirit to the whole construct. Since the 1960s this condition of architecture has held a magic for some of the more adventurous of designers. Intriguingly, we will discover that Lim's work is subject to the same forensic attention to the detail of joints, parts and layers as to the issue of the good-old straightforward juxtaposition that is necessary in the composition of static buildings. Metamorphosis of built or constructed form exists, at the conceptual level, as a parallel explosion to that of the impact of high technology and the digital world on architecture. Yet we can also observe that as a form of 'advanced five-finger exercise' it enables one to dismember, reconsider, reconfigure, dismember again and so on several times. The preferred configuration may not be the last in the series. So have we returned to a very advanced equivalent of the sculptor's turntable?

In a piece of work that is considered over several months, its strategy is probably mulled over a number of times and the drawn version deliberately set with a task – in parallel with other tasks undertaken by other subsets

CJ Lim, Soho Threshold: Wardour St Old Compton St, Soho, London, UK, 1995. Ink on film.

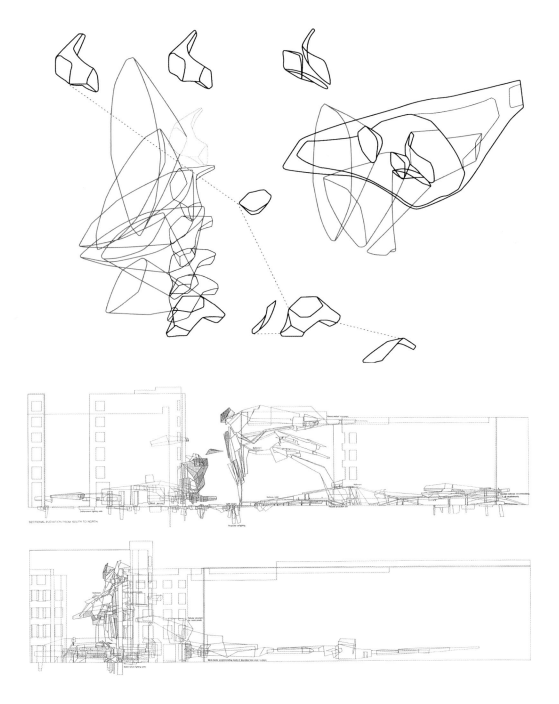

SECTIONAL ELEVATION FROM SOUTH TO NORTH

of drawings. This was certainly the case in the Way Out West–Berlin project that I made in the late 1980s. It was in response to the invitation by Kristin Feireiss, director of Berlin's Aedes gallery to 40 or so people to make a project for Berlin.

I feed in this peripheral information to make a point about drawings and incentive. A very high proportion of the drawings in this book were made for competitions, as book or publicity illustrations, and either directly for exhibition, or highly conscious that they would be exhibited at some time. The question, then, concerns the nature of the audience.

Peter Cook, Way Out West–Berlin, 1988. Layout of district (adjoining Hallensee): early stage. Ink and coloured pencil, 60 x 75 cm.

As with the submission drawings for a competition one is talking to other architects, here in Berlin one was talking to a very particular set of architects: with Lebbeus Woods, Daniel Libeskind, Zaha Hadid and Thom Mayne on the list, one was in 'fast company'. Yet essentially the project was also giving birth to a set of combinations of generic type, substance and formation that were new to the author and not to be found elsewhere. The setting up of a grid upon a curious corner of West Berlin was an essential first move. Then the establishment of an internal language of built blocks,

Peter Cook, Way Out West–Berlin, 1988. Layout of district (adjoining Hallensee): later stage. Ink and coloured pencil, 60 x 75 cm.

Peter Cook, Way Out West–Berlin, 1988. Park and tunnel. Ink and watercolour with small areas of coloured pencil: 60 x 60 cm.

Peter Cook, Way Out West–Berlin, 1988. Typical corner (section/elevation): early stage. Ink and watercolour with small areas of coloured pencil, 60 x 60 cm.

Peter Cook, Way Out West–Berlin, 1988. Typical corner (section/elevation): later stage. Ink and watercolour with small areas of coloured pencil, 60 x 60 cm.

WAY OUT WEST - BERLIN - STAGE E

1   100   200

PETER COOK
1988

pods, armatures, swathes of planting and wilder vegetation along with a key, wayward element: the 'cactus'. These had to pass through a number of stages at which the role played by each would shift, the hierarchies exchanging and the forms mutating.

At this, the western end of the wonderful Kurfürstendamm, the no-man's-land behind the Halensee lake would erupt into a giant hybrid of building and growths. Essential was the description of the sequence: punctuated by continuous instances of the formal rearrangements – strange though they might be. An introductory diagram set the scene and introduced the cactus. Then the sequence of five plans: the stages of development or metamorphosis. A matter-of-fact technique is enough: black lines, coloured inks, pencil-crayoned or pencil-shaded surfaces. The generating lines carry on from the instigation of the city fragment as a simple 'American' downtown towards something not a little reminiscent of the Arizona desert.

It did not seem necessary or appropriate to use exactly the same drawing technique for elevations and sections, which were anyhow taken at two larger scales. At the largest scale a fragment is shown at two stages of metamorphosis: the first while the components are still identifiable as products of a rectangular frame system, the second at the point where the 'cactus influence' is really under way. At a smaller scale, the same phases described in the plans are seen in section, but the drawing technique for all these drops coloured ink in favour of watercolour as the infill. All the drawings start off as ink lines with the larger drawings photocopied onto watercolour paper.

So little has been left to chance and all the work in this chapter, though broadly 'experimental', is mature work, where the authors have made earlier experiments and have a clear idea of the line of trajectory, and where the strategy is premeditated. The observer merely needs to spend sufficient time to read and follow the sequence.

3

Drawing and Vision

In this chapter I deal with a set of works that, through their uniqueness – one might almost say their 'confrontational' quality – the detail features (though they may very well be there) are almost unimportant. To what extent the mode of the drawing is contributory to this confrontation is debatable. Certainly in none of the examples is there a conflict with the spirit of the piece. Certainly there may be other drawings or models (or in some cases here, the actual building itself) that do an equally valid job of conveying the spirit, but another issue is at hand.

To what extent both vision and drawing are intrinsically creations of the moment and to what extent they confront the rest of the architectural culture of that moment becomes easier to measure as we become distanced in time. In the case of Otto Wagner, there was clearly an agreed method for the making of perspectives and of elevations. The publication some years ago of the work of Wagner's students at the Vienna Academy of Fine Arts indicates a tightly imposed set of procedures. The importance of detail is particular to this work: the more because it was not the traditional Renaissance version of the classical *parti*. It was inventive, to some extent reductive, and then exploded into bold composition and exotic morsels of decoration or, rather, applied art.

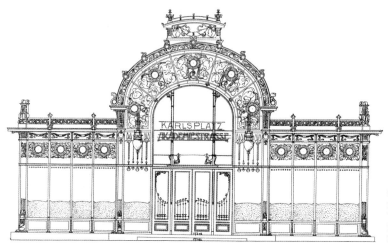

Otto Wagner, Karlsplatz
Station, Vienna, Austria,
1898–9. Archives of the Wiener
Stadtwerke-Verkehrsbetriebe,
Stadtbahn map No 860.

Viennese Visionaries

The elevation of the Karlsplatz Station on the Vienna loop line (built 1898–
99) demands of the draughtsman a degree of precision as well as articulation
that must be carried out fully if it is to do justice to its very sophisticated
set of intentions. A partial vision would be insufficient for the sheer control
of aesthetic that is carried out in this relatively small building. More than
a century later it remains as a pavilion of the status of a Greek temple or
the Petit Trianon at Versailles, despite its utilitarian role as a commuter
station. That there was such a developed system of tectonic notation as that
produced in the Wagner office is phenomenon enough. The existence of the
very well-maintained object alongside does not detract from the view that
formal drawing of buildings had reached a very high moment at that time.

Somehow one cannot escape Austria in any survey of the haunting or the
exquisite in architectural drawing. Hans Hollein is at once a rebel and a
questioner: it is he who declaimed 'everything is architecture' and then made
several series of projects that invoked everyday objects as a replacement
for architecture. Pills, sunglasses, inflatables, wheeled vehicles and then,
ultimately, an aircraft carrier as the counteraction to the conventional city
(see his Aircraft Carrier City in Landscape, 1964). Only Claes Oldenburg
might claim, through his giant lipstick and other juxtapositions, the role of
arch collagist-provocateur. Yet Hollein places the carrier on the Austrian
countryside with the full knowledge that, though absurd, the nature of this

particular vessel is that it houses the equivalent of a small town and a fleet of aircraft. The fact that they are boxed up in an immediately recognisable but complete object, and that it is not jumping scale (as does the Oldenburg), adds piquancy to the affront. In fact you just about *could* do such a thing and it just about *could* work.

Technically, too, the collage is sufficiently homogeneous that this secondary (and worrisome) level of confrontation is maintained. To students of Hollein and his friend, architect, artist, assembler and draughtsman Walter Pichler, the memory of their fascination with complete-figure cities and Inca cities also comes into play. (For more on Pichler and his work, see the beginning of Chapter 8.) An aircraft carrier is indeed the complete city-figure.

The 20th-Century City-Figure

In a sense there are three such figurations that stem from the mid-20th century: Hollein's piece, the Unité d'Habitation by Le Corbusier, captured in Nadir Afonso's famous image of 1946, and Archigram member Ron Herron's Walking City (1964). All three are compacted and transferable. Indeed, Le Corbusier built four Unité d'Habitation housing units in France – Marseilles, Nantes, Briey and Firminy – and one in Berlin. Herron's Walking City (or 'Cities Moving' to cite the original title) is depicted in various drawings as being alongside New York, in the desert or in the ocean. Though the person who enjoyed the business of drawing almost more than anyone else, for his Walking City on the Ocean (1966) Herron was sufficiently well organised to prepare standard (drawn) components. He then had them reproduced, and collaged these pieces together to form the body and legs. Certain bespoke elements were then drawn in and the total object could be re-photographed up or down to form the family of objects. The final piece of collage drawing concerned the setting.

Hans Hollein, Aircraft Carrier City in Landscape, 1964. Perspective: collage. Museum of Modern Art, New York.

Most people viewing this immensely powerful image are uninterested in the process of its creation, yet it suggests, again, a certain connection between the created image and the idea of ubiquitousness.

Vision Intensified

A vision of a quite different kind obsessed Austrian architect Günther Domenig for many years. Having built up an international reputation as both an 'iconic' architect of smaller buildings and as a reliable creator of large buildings, he was determined to create a special piece on a plot of inherited land alongside Lake Ossiach near Klagenfurt. This was inspired by the geometries of the rocks on the mountains behind the site, and was at the extreme point of the geometries that his experimental works had been edging towards. The Steinhaus (Stonehouse) (1986) became his marker, his shrine to architecture. The drawings for it are fulsome evocations of all the skill and the fine 'eye' that Domenig brings to bear upon his work. A close friend of Walter Pichler and sharing some of the same mannerisms

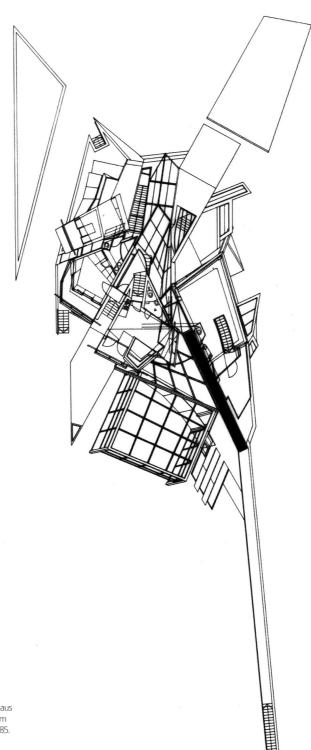

Günther Domenig, Steinhaus
(Stonehouse), Steindor am
Ossiacher See, Austria, 1985.
Second-floor plan.

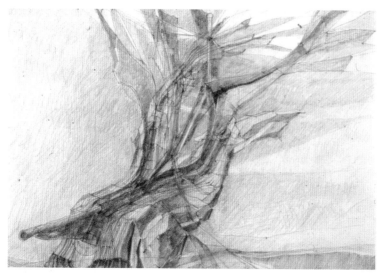

Günther Domenig, The Tree or The Branching Out, Steinhaus (Stonehouse), Steindorf am Ossiacher See, Austria, 1986. Sketch (1980): pencil and coloured pencil.

in his freehand sketches, Domenig's Steinhaus drawings are an intriguing combination of that intense, Austrian pencil mannerism – where you can almost feel the intensity of the pencilled stroke – and the wish to be very specific about the positioning and the sculpting of the piece.

In certain respects, this intensity directs us more clearly than the built building: it holds onto the vision while only occurring on a piece of white paper, whereas the house, though finely executed, is subject to its surroundings, the time of day, the state of the materials in wet or dry weather and the like. So we have another paradox: that the drawn building is more pure, more concentrated than the built building. Is the latter the *real* thing but the former the *true* thing? A tricky question.

The Genesis of Vision

Creating a 'vision' can be a developed skill. It can even be applied to architecture that may not be in the first rank in terms of either originality or technique – or in beauty or skill of composition. One wonders how many commercial proposals for New York skyscrapers were passed across the drawing board of American delineator and architect Hugh Ferriss during the 1930s and how much licence he was permitted in his re-creation of them as true 'visions'? (See his drawing here of the Fisher Building for Detroit of 1927.) A brilliantly developed technique and the deliberate restriction of

Hugh Ferriss, Fisher Building, Detroit, Michigan, US, 1927. Photomechanical reproduction on paper.

intense light and shadow (particularly the latter) meant that his towering masses could celebrate the awesomeness of the tall, mountainous solids. His mountains had none of the 'locality', nostalgia or fine grain of Domenig's stones; they were much more abstract, much more designed to impress – in a general kind of way. Yet haunting. Tempting. Near to the dream of the great city, yet, with their well-considered setbacks, based on the daylighting laws, immediately tangible through their relationship to the known, the real, the regular.

Zaha Hadid, Phaeno Science
Centre, Wolfsburg, Germany,
2006. Computer rendering
(2000).

To what extent Zaha Hadid's epoch-making vision of Hong Kong had to be
as formulaic as Ferriss, or as intense as Domenig, has not needed to be put
to the test. The Peak, planned as a spa for the city and the winning entry in a
watershed competition in 1983, was never built, but its urban vision and the
notion of her building as yet another – if special – outcrop makes a wonderful
statement about urbanism (see also Chapter 6). It suggests that beyond the
brilliance of the sweeping curves and cantilevers of the building itself lies a
city of exuberant outcropping, quite possibly able to absorb more wonderful
sweeping or thrusting structures. The whole island is a conglomerate of
built and carved form whereby mud and steel, concrete and glass, road and
funicular are but shared elements of the total outcropping.

It is a very optimistic vision, establishing the role of architecture in a totally
positive way. Almost denying the need for man-made urbanity to make
any unnecessary concessions to nature or found terrain. It comes at a
point in Hadid's career when her process of drawing had developed into
a sophisticated sequence of both elimination and augmentation. With
confident lines and clear coloration; with an establishment of clear priorities
and a team of assistants who were, by now, trained to perform precisely,
respecting the genius of the engineer, Peter Rice, and believing in the
heroicism of the sculpted solid. These same confident lines can be found
in her later work, carrying with them her discovery of a more voluptuous
physiognomy such as that in the Phaeno Science Centre in Wolfsburg,
Germany (2006).

Zaha Hadid, The Peak, Hong
Kong, 1982–3. Exploded
isometric: painting, acrylic on
board.

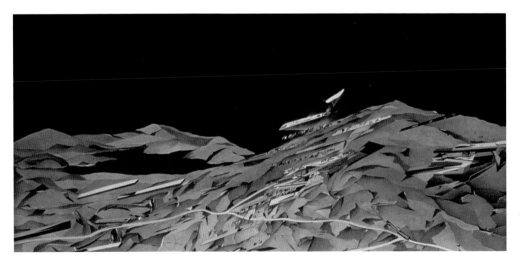

For many years, the question raised by the Steinhaus drawings – that the drawing might hold the 'truth' of an architecture – had to suffice in relation to Hadid's work. This and the many other drawings had established a credential, but the public always wanted to see the flesh. Weaker, jealous designers would always predict that when she did build, there would be an enormous denouement. Subsequent history has denied them the pleasure of this prediction. So we can return now to an equivocal state between Hadid's drawings and her formed forms and probably return again and again to the conundrum.

Drawing as Statement

Certain architects step beyond the purely architectural in their referencing and their inspiration, making the assembly of parts or of figure the servant of other impulses. Considering the visionary potential of inventions on paper as a form of script or programme is a statement or viewpoint which, if anything, places an even greater pressure on the components of the drawing to be articulate, or at least to be carefully chosen; whereas the designer-drawer sets up a motivation, often knowing his or her criteria, almost by instinct, and the detail parts come forth on the wing of an idea. So the more cerebral approach is more demanding – and often less successful. One of the most thoughtful makers of drawings (as well as large-scale installations) is

Melvin Charney, The Other City: Visions of the Temple No 1, 1986. Pastel on paper (arches: 100% cotton, 185 gsm), 92.2 x 125.7 cm. The Canadian Centre for Architecture.

Elia Zenghelis and Zoe Zenghelis,
Hotel Sphinx, New York, US,
1975–6. Axonometric: synthetic
polymer paint and ink on paper,
46.7 x 55.9 cm. Museum of
Modern Art, New York.

Canadian Melvin Charney who avoids stagnation through his sophistication
as an artist-architect (see, for example, his The Other City: Visions of the
Temple No 1, 1986). His visual referencing is very wide and he can parry the
intellectual discrimination by a pictorial instinct that kicks in just in time. His
work intrigues one, again, because it sets up a tantalising vision of near-
reality, but with a clear distance between the imagery and true reality.

The British Greek-born architects Elia and Zoe Zenghelis caught us in the
same territory, but with quite a definitive architectural object, during the
early years of the Office for Metropolitan Architecture (OMA). Hotel Sphinx
(1975–6), suggested for Times Square in New York City, is immediately
arresting because of its original figuration, but also because the drawing itself

presents the hotel object as the total statement. The road pattern is drawn, but in the most abstracted way and in near-monochrome, whereas the hotel is pink, blue, orange and black with enough detail to keep one amused, up and down the two flights that make up the composition. In a single image, the notion of the luxurious icon is resurrected in the role of styled elements.

Through such a formula, the fact that the mannerisms of the smaller parts speak very much of the period, it is the élan (or even 'cuteness') of the drawing that lives on beyond its period. It serves to remind us of the range of culture, the range of manner, during the latter part of the 20th century.

If Sphinx was parrying with a hedonistic world with an exuberance of manner, Cedric Price's environment of the Potteries, near to his birthplace in Staffordshire, becomes the recipient of good, healthy medicine administered with the astringent wit that we have come to expect. Instead of an abstracted location we have a very specific world of rail yards, slag heaps and scruffy marginal land. The strategy of the Potteries Thinkbelt (1964–6), designed with the planner, Peter Hall, involves the placing of a form of university on railway carriages so that it can be reconfigured and grow dynamically. The cartoon-like indications of gantries, tanks, carriages, cars, decks or housing seem fully sufficient, not only in order to illustrate the logic of the programme, but, more tellingly, to remind us of a certain astringent, brooding atmosphere that is at the same time down to earth. At the time, its publication in the weekly *New Society* (a serious but relatively popular sociology journal) had the character of a major statement. It is another vision that has not been dulled by time – remaining a major contribution to both urban theory and any discussion about physical or academic resources. Yet one can only speculate on the manner in which it might have been presented 30, 20 or even 10 years later. We have become accustomed to such proposals being presented in a more elaborate way, certainly in colour, almost certainly with attempts to beautify the surroundings and quite likely couched in easily digestible vignettes of student life, fun with trains, and friendly Staffordshire folk.

The starkness, the clarity of the idea and the essentiality of the drawings leave no glib escape routes for the faint-hearted. We are in the hands of serious thinkers.

Not that urban escape can necessarily come to the unsuspecting public. Among the visionary drawings of architects it is fascinating to remind

Cedric Price, Potteries, Thinkbelt,
Staffordshire, UK, 1964-6.
Perspective of Madeley Transfer
Area Staffordshire, UK: ink and
white ink on selectively abraded
gelatin silver print, mounted on
board with self-adhesive paper
dots, 18.4 x 36.5 cm.

Perspective of Battery, Sprawl
and Capsule Housing, Hanley
Site Staffordshire, UK: ink and
crayon on selectively abraded
gelatin silver prints, mounted on
board, 16.2 x 42.9 cm.

Erich Kettelhut,
Morgendämmerung (Dawn),
Germany, 1926. Oil on cardboard,
48.3 x 65.0 cm.

ourselves of the impact that architecture can have when manipulated by
a scenic artist such as Erich Kettelhut, who was one of the designers on
Fritz Lang's film *Metropolis* (1927). His Morgendämmerung (Dawn) of 1926
confronts us with the accumulated impact of towers of building that, unlike
Hugh Ferriss' circumspect piles, are jostling together and almost climbing up
on each other towards a sky that is only just not on fire! The large areas of
brooding (or is it threatening?) black add to the orchestration. This piece of
silent Wagnerian heroism is achieved without any very special architectural
features. Close scrutiny reveals some commonplace strips and bays with
repetitive windows.

Cedric Price, Potteries Thinkbelt,
Staffordshire, UK, 1964–6.
Perspective of Mobile Teaching
Machines: self-adhesive printed
polymer sheets with ink and
graphite on tracing paper, with
self-adhesive paper dots, 31.1 x
27.9 cm.

Here and there are hints of the north German Expressionism of Hugo Häring
or of Fritz Höger's Chilehaus in Hamburg. All incorporated and absorbed into
a brilliantly 'stagy' evocation of the might of the future city.

Einstein Tower, 1920–21. Photo
taken c. 1930.

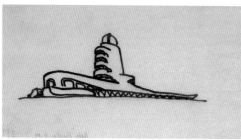

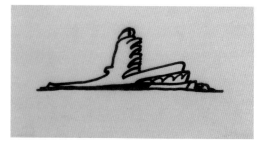

Erich Mendelsohn, Sketches
of the Einstein Tower,
Potsdam, Germany, undated.
Kunstbibliothek, Staatliche
Museum zu Berlin, HdZ EM
5149/1-3.

Vision and impact clearly do not always need the support of original detail.

This last statement can be turned on its side to support an architecture that, by definition, needs little detail: that almost eschews detail.

The drawings proceeding from it take advantage of such intention. They are on the borderline of being under-informed, yet have immense power. The architecture of Erich Mendelsohn was the product of a virtuoso sense of directionality as well as a clear sense of compositional priorities. It zaps along with the miniature sketches containing almost all you need for the Einstein Tower at Potsdam (1920–21). It is necessary here to glance at a photograph of the actual building to underscore the point. We can go on to discuss the material issue of making an object that is as pure in image as the drawing – but having to make it out of a rough old accumulation of components and concealments.

After all, if the drawing is not to lead the way, what else?

Le Corbusier's sketches, now somehow associated with the insistent power and mythology that surround an architect of unparalleled influence, might surely be expected to have the same detachment as those of Mendelsohn.

Le Corbusier, Carthage, Tunisia: Villa Baizeau, 1928. Gelatin print on thick paper, 55 x 104 cm. Fondation Le Corbusier.

Peter Cook (with Christine
Hawley and Gerry Whale),
Sponge City, 1975. Painted acrylic
panels with a small area of
collage, 1250 x 260 cm.

Certainly he was more than equal in self-confidence and chutzpah. Certainly the emergent architecture was without compromise. Certainly the drawings were very personal and have all the flavour of the work itself. Yet, if the interior of Villa Baizeau in Carthage, Tunisia (1928) is to be a guide, they are full of 'humanising' elements. Opened books, casual cushions, a plant in a pot, a modest sailing boat in the water, the inhabitants chatting on the bedroom balcony.

Even the concrete is specked to indicate light and shade – or is it to indicate substance? It is as if the Master himself was trying to be both bold and at the same time, reassuring.

Visionary drawing does not stand outside the basic scheme of architectural development – it just, sometimes, wants to make a leap forward.

In my own Sponge City (1975) I sought to demonstrate how a landscape and a series of tectonic moves can combine to make architecture. Different from that which we have in a fairly obvious sense: in that the combination suggested was somewhat exotic. Different from that which we have in the sense of its scatter – its dependence on a matrix in places which then just merges into the foliated mass. Out of this comes a hybrid between a berry and a capsule. Elsewhere there are lines of transparent skin – or is it window? But these too are able to merge into the foliated condition.

As various as the component elements were the methods of drawing – involving painting and collage. The painters were Christine Hawley and Gerry Whale, both able to use the brush more effectively than myself, though following the rules set up by an earlier, much smaller version that was drawn and watercoloured. This, in turn, followed a programme for the piece, drawn as part diagram, part picture.

The final 4-metre-long piece has a visionary quality and the two lead-up pictures have a more diagrammatic quality. This set of comparative and possibly interdependent approaches sets yet another conundrum regarding motive as well as vision.

Might there be a graphical imperative? Is one visionary definition that of the scale of attack? Sometimes it seems to be so.

4

Drawing and Image

So far, the assumption has been made that when we are consciously looking at an architectural drawing we are confirming certain assumptions about the presence of buildings, their condition as objects in space, and that somewhere along the line the thing that we are looking at links with our experience of inhabiting buildings. However distant from our day-to-day experience some of these examples are, there is a resonance.

There are detachments that accumulate, so that a piece of work can have reminiscences of sets of expectations, but then set up so many deviations that (depending upon our receptivity) we suspend our systems. Maybe we just lie back and enjoy. Maybe we are suspicious but go along with it anyhow, carried along by the same suspension with which we are fascinated by a spooky film, the musical move from a familiar to a dissonant chord, the strange turn in a narrative.

Choosing the Means and Transcending the Medium

In such a way we can confront Free Architecture: House for Three Families (1981), a drawing by the Japanese architect Masaharu Takasaki, an advocate of cosmological architecture. Momentarily we cling on to a profile, another clue or a hint of a change in surface or an orifice. The colour, too, is near-reality for a building, but still somehow in the world of drawing-as-drawing. Yet if we know Takasaki's work and look back several years before to his

Masaharu Takasaki, Free
Architecture: House for Three
Families, 1981. Drawing paper,
coloured pencil and pencil,
21 x 29.5 cm.

Shinkenchiku Residential Design Competition proposal of 1977 with its title
Confusion, we can surmise that the confusion has at least been resolved. The
later drawing is no mere diagram, but a working-out of ideas for a building.

Those who know his work will recognise that Takasaki is a genuine formal
experimenter and that the drawings mentioned here are the early moments
in proposing a genuinely new architecture: choosing a means of drawing *only
as necessary* and moving straight into the investigation itself.

The work of Santa Monica-based Morphosis has been consistently exposed
to a world audience from the earliest days of the practice's small houses in
Venice, California, of the 1970s, until founder Thom Mayne's triumphal entry
into New York and Paris with the Cooper Union New Academic Building
(due for completion in 2008) and the Phare Tower, La Défense, France
(construction of which began in 2007). These were demonstrated to the
press via almost simultaneous exposures of models: generated and placed on
paper or computer cut in touchable material. Their development, too, owes
so much to the to-and-fro of editing and decision making that it genuinely
transcends the medium, leaving a discussion of Mayne's drawings either to

Morphosis, Rendering of Phare Tower, La Défense, Paris, France, 2007.

Morphosis, Rendering of Atrium study, Cooper Union New Academic Building, New York, US, 2005 (due for completion in 2008).

a deliberate rear view or to an examination of motive, vision, strategy and image – as one. His approach to architecture is known and highly respected. He appears to agonise – but in a very positive way – towards the validation and re-examination of projects. He criticises and teaches with unusual thoroughness. Equally, his position vis-à-vis drawing has at times been quite heroic. He was among the first professors to insist that his whole class should work only with computers. He was ready to turn away from the delightful mannerisms of the earlier Morphosis models of the 1980s, with their encrustation of palette-knife surfaces and rich orchestration.

Nonetheless, Morphosis projects have always been capable of thorough examination in plan, nearly always containing virtuoso moments for the connoisseur to enjoy. Such plans need only a straightforward mode of drawing: the direct outline that sufficed from the 1950s to, say, 1995, and was best produced by the Japanese, Germans, English and Swiss – who avoided the pencil and went straight for the crisp ink line. Examine any project out of, say, the Technical University of Darmstadt in that period and you have to acknowledge the essential lack of ambiguity that is inbuilt.

The computer has effortlessly moved in on this territory and it is almost impossible, in the best work, to distinguish one from the other. Indeed, it is pointless to try. The end intention is the critical issue: to place elements and intersections precisely, to take measure of them, to support strategy by local decisiveness.

The work of Morphosis subscribes to this. Thus we can compare the imagery of two distinct periods of the practice's work and compare 'picture' drawing with straight plan. With a sufficient background in the evaluation of placement, this business of precision has its most apparently 'spatial' imagery thoroughly developed out of worked sequences. Where the hand stopped pulling a pen across the sheet and a series of electronic impulses took over is almost incidental.

The simple idea of a 'very thin house' was both a provocation and a self-imposed exercise in which an acknowledged expert in the statement of surface and atmosphere could bring this expertise to bear upon the idea. Raimund Abraham's House without Rooms (1974–5) became the stranger through its combination of drawn physicality and peculiarity. A more abstracted surface might have distanced the whole thing from us and lost the sense of tangible curiousness from the project.

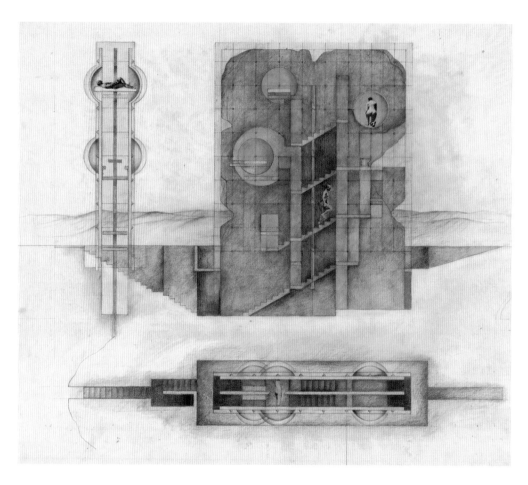

Raimund Abraham, The House without Rooms, 1974–5. Elevation and plan: coloured pencil, graphite and cut-and-pasted printed paper on paper, 87.9 x 96.8 cm, not signed, not dated. Museum of Modern Art, New York.

Its author is the product of the Austrian school of incisive drawing already hinted at in the introduction of the work of Hans Hollein and Günther Domenig in Chapter 3. If Walter Pichler has not needed to take on the full professional role as an architect, but has been able to push the genre further than the rest, it is Abraham who has most assiduously developed its atmospherics. There is a curious link between his technique and that of American experimental architect and artist Lebbeus Woods (see his work reproduced in Chapters 6, 8 and 9), whereby the grain and patina of the material and the brooding quality of a shadow come to bear upon the already visible challenge of the profile (or circumstance) of an object. The thin house is usually read as both plan and section. An interesting exercise

Aldo Rossi, Palazzo della Regione, Trieste, Italy, 1974. Studio drawing of the interior and exterior perspective. Deutsches Architekturmuseum Collection, Frankfurt/Main.

is to separate them and try to imagine the range of implications available from only the one or the other.

Mannerism

For me the section and plan of the thin house are independently provocative, leading to another issue, which is as much to do with drawn mannerism as anything else. For me, the work of the Italian architect and designer Aldo Rossi remained (except for one or two late and surprisingly commercial-looking buildings) a provocation. Arch in its Rationalism, provocative in its avoidance of anything that hinted at Modernism or anything suggesting a condition of 'flow', its manners were those of the reinforcement of a grounded, sober and predominantly solid architecture. The features reduced to the sanctity of an early Christian church – or more. The vibrations recalling the solidity of stone buildings arising out of parched soil.

It is hard for a late Modernist free-former from the tradition of the North Sea to sympathise with such mannerism. My instinctive responses are to the wind, the waves and the pull of the vessel upon the ropes, the bolting and locking of metal and the making of machines as a re-evocation of that spirit. Thus my reaction to Rossi's drawings is of a bewildered bystander. Yet in stating this

I am offering them a certain type of respect. They ooze certainty. They defy one to shy away. In terms of imagery, they are unequivocal.

Stemming from a certain and established cultural line, the Rossi work featured here could be insistent without being shrill, which was a luxury denied the architects of the Russian Revolution. Called upon to celebrate the new Soviet culture, the young Russians of the early 20th century drew with a fascinating combination of verve and nonchalance without the latter destroying the power of their work, particularly in emblematic terms. If we dwell for too long upon Ilya Golosov's drawings (made in competition) for the USSR Pavilion for the 1925 Exposition Internationale des Arts Décoratifs et Industriels Modernes in Paris, we might find that they lack the finesse of most of those we have seen so far. Instead, there is a sense of exuberance and urgency. The simple suggestion of planar surfaces and big, bold emblems carried by them, with a graphic simplicity of the windows that works well with the general composition, serves as an introduction to a new stage of Modernism where, in fact, it could begin to enjoy itself and enjoy colour as well.

Ilya Golosov, USSR Pavilion for the 1925 Exposition des Arts Décoratifs et Industriels Modernes, Paris, France, 1925. Elevations (1924): ink, coloured ink and watercolour on paper, 22.9 x 33.1 cm.

We shall see more Soviet work that reiterates this overt enthusiasm, seen from different directions of impact (Iakov Chernikov's Architectural Fantasy in Chapter 6, and Ivan Léonidov's Commissariat of Heavy Industry in Chapter 7). Drawn or composed by differing temperaments, this seems to have been a shared experience and, if it is categorised as a mannerism, one can only applaud it all.

Paper Architecture

The spirit of Russian Constructivism and much of its imagery carried on in the minds of Elia Zenghelis, Rem Koolhaas and Zaha Hadid in their early work, seemed to have harmed them very little. Modern Russia seems to have both a love and hate relationship to it, perhaps for its political resonance, yet one quite respectably democratic Russian, Yuri Avvakumov, seems to have captured and continued its spirit as well as its imagery. The 1970s and 1980s experienced the emergence of the so-called 'paper architects' in Russia – none of whom had the chance to build, but they drew and drew. Cut off from most of the Western experimentalists, their work carried with it a certain heroicism that demanded of it a high degree of imagery. Very much abstracted from the need to build, it was poetic and slightly winsome in character. Gradually it filtered out into the Western world via Finland.

Its cultural context and, perhaps, the fascination of its detachment, led to its central position in the 1970s and 1980s discussions of the creative role of drawn architecture as opposed to built architecture. About this time there emerged a series of architecture galleries in such cities as Berlin, London, Munich, Hamburg, Oslo, Copenhagen, Toronto, Paris and New York (at the time of writing, only the Aedes in Berlin and the Storefront in New York have survived and remain highly influential). The architecture world and a wing of the art world started to comment that while built architecture was becoming predictable, there was a spirit to be found in paper architecture and with it a plethora of images.

Then the 1990s developed as a period in which many of the paper architects began to build and prove that their extension of the vocabulary of architecture could be applied. Many of the drawings in this book are by those who were at one time influential as 'unbuilt' or 'drawing' architects before they started to build (I know, I was one of them). The effect on the galleries has been mixed, with drawings being published in newspapers for visualisation purposes to reveal to a general public a proposal for a likely

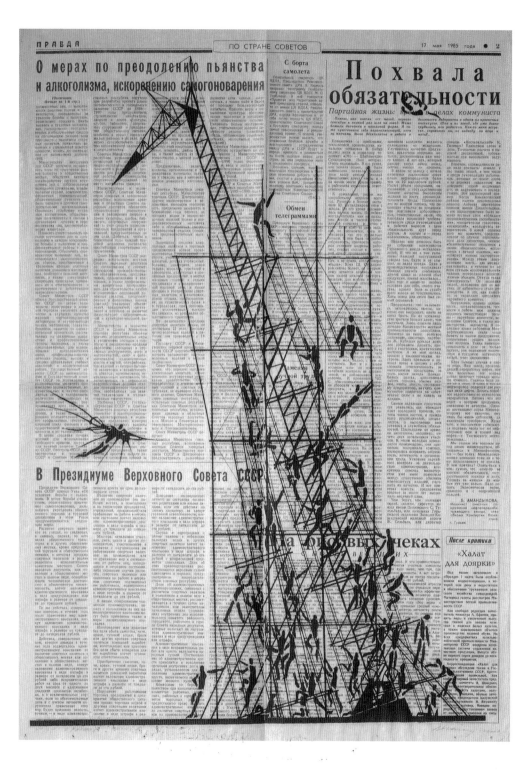

О мерах по преодолению пьянства и алкоголизма, искоренению самогоноварения

С борта самолета

Похвала обязательности

Партийная жизнь: долг в делах коммуниста

Обмен телеграммами

В Президиуме Верховного Совета СССР

После критики

«Халат для доярки»

Б. АМАНДЫКОВА.

Yuri Avvakumov and Yuri Kuzin, Red Tower (Homage to Vladimir Tatlin), 1986–9. Silkscreen print on newspaper.

building. This has pulled back the contemplation of serious innovation into the coteries: the schools of architecture or the reviewers of competitions.

Imagery as Imagery

Nonetheless, the search continues for new architecture that is not restricted by either client demand or academic exercise. The territory of discovery has shifted to the digital mode. Much is said and written about the self-generation that can emanate from the digitised examination of topology and cellular aggregations. At best, this results in an imagery that can be extremely exotic and formally beyond anything seen before, so that a project such as the PS1 MoMA Pavilion, New York (2005) by LA-based Argentinian Hernán Díaz Alonso can, in his own words, 'work with scripts and particles … and can be used afterwards as a laboratory for where we want to go next'.

Alonso describes some of his work as to do with the problem of the sublime. By introducing such instigations and such objectives, he points out the advantage of this work in terms of its speed and range. Yet it is immediately clear that a designer of such skill is still in command of the search. The wish to disengage the criteria and methodology of such work from the tradition of drawing and redrawing is not necessary, though it is sometimes stated as

Hernán Díaz Alonso, PS1 MoMA Pavilion, New York, US, 2005. Animation-based software, 720 x 486 pixels.

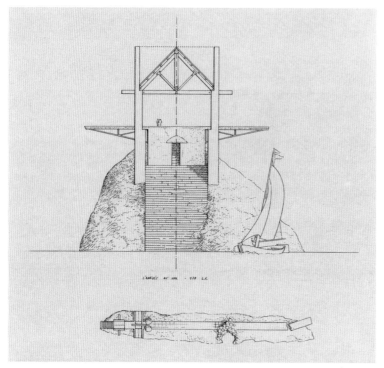

Léon Krier, House for Rita, 1974. Perspective and plan: ink on paper, 20.9 x 20.9 cm. Museum of Modern Art, New York.

a form of battle cry by the religiously pro-digital. Díaz Alonso, though quite young, nonetheless comes from the direction of designing rather than theory. His imagery is imagery and can exist printed on to a flat piece of paper if you wish. For my purposes it is a drawing, in the sense that it is the visual statement of an idea. It is a drawing in the sense that a solid object is being suggested and codified.

In their spirit of formal challenge such drawings are described as the by-products of the manipulation of the form. The manipulation is edited and directed towards certain ends and inevitably contains physical and formal prejudices. The excitement of it lies in its creative optimism and largesse. This contrasts with the simplicity of the early work of Luxembourg-born architect Léon Krier, now best known for his part in designing the Prince of Wales's model town of Poundbury in Dorset. This depended on a narrowing of the focus and a reductive language. One would not expect Krier to wish for the same sublime as Díaz Alonso, though the piquancy of an image such as that for the House for Rita (1974) – his then wife – does suggest another sublime.

It is deliberately archaic. It is deliberately imperfect. It inhabits a preciously small island. Yet its fairytale quality cannot conceal the very architectural dogmatism that is the vehicle for the sublimation.

Though it is at the other end of the scale, the perspective here of the Lower Manhattan Expressway (1972) by Paul Rudolph, the architect of the Yale Art and Architecture Building, exudes a rather similar perfected detachment from the muddle of the real city. The strength of the imagery is, as in most of the other cases, to do with the consistency of manner, and in particular the consistency of geometry: spicily stacked and focused in, onto the Expressway itself. The image is determinedly architectural: a complete concrete world. Close inspection will reveal some trees, patternings and flags, but these are never allowed to deflect from the perfection of the scene.

Paul Rudolph, Lower Manhattan Expressway, New York, US, 1972. Perspective to the east: ink and graphite on paper, 101.6 x 85.1 cm. Museum of Modern Art, New York.

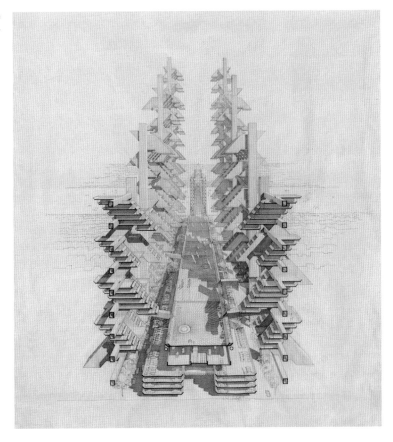

The complete world and the single aesthetic are very much bound up within the tradition of the guiding image in architecture. Almost as a religious rite, the exclusion of counter-aesthetics, the limitation of eccentric mannerisms, the reiteration of gambits within a single picture all speak of the insistence that is deemed necessary to this tradition. Historically, therefore, we bounce back and forth between image and counter-image – and further counter-image – thus leaving the process of absorption and the merging of parts of one with the other to the mainstream imitators for whom the pure and heady models such as these are too strong.

Concentration can incorporate romance, however. Despite its origins as a commercial project, the fully 'treed' warehouse for Best Products gave James Wines of SITE the opportunity to indulge in one of his favourite gambits: that of the vegetated building. The drawings have been made with such authenticity that the result is certainly delightful. What could have been a corny idea is, like an expert piece of knitting, exactly tuned and seems – though eccentric – comfortably viable. One feels that any other form of representation or even the use of colour would have lost the charm and sublimeness of the idea.

Thought-Through Technique: Ensnaring Spontaneity

At this point, one looks into the matter of technique to establish just when and why a certain idea has to be captured at the right degree of explicitness. One would like to think that a strong image needs no subtlety of interpretation, but it is not always so.

James Wines, BEST Forest Showroom, Richmond, Virginia, US, 1980. Perspective (1978): pen and ink on paper, 34.6 x 43.2 cm. Collection FRAC Centre, Orléans.

The initial power of a drawing can often come from the moves that result in the juxtaposition of parts. The author holds certain objectives in his or her head and knows that they can be developed: the key, however, is to relate them together. It is no accident that the word 'plan' has come to be used in a general sense for every type of enterprise from war through crime to seduction: very often implying a sequence of operations, but also tending to centralise around a single documentation of the strategy involved. True that in architecture we will produce layers of plans at various levels, but still tend to feature one of them as the representative of the main thrust of the idea.

At the École des Beaux-Arts in Paris during the 19th century, a highly sophisticated tradition was established in which a variety of rules and gambits could be applied to the layout of buildings. As the tradition developed, these became more and more mannered and increasingly clever. The ability to make use of interstitial spaces and odd corners, and the delight in changing from the orthogonal geometry to the diagonal, led to a plethora of cute devices such as the incorporation of small oval or circular rooms at the crotch of the geometrical shift, or the carving out of odd niche-like spaces. A foreknowledge of the implications of all this for the making of domes or vaults was implicit. A total image of the building might well be that of the progression of the plan towards the sum of its construct – as with a Romantic symphony of the same period.

Shadow House (1980) by British architect and professor Christine Hawley stems in part from the same set of references: the development of its ideas centralised on the single plan drawing. (I myself became involved at a later stage in the development of a model of the same project, as well as being responsible for some minor bits and pieces on the plan.) The manner of the architecture was essentially scenographic and very much to do with the incorporation of waterfalls, rocks, a form of 'tempietto' and the softening of the edges between the 'hard' – or geometrically identifiable – elements and the surrounding ground and gardens. More than this, the notion was that of a construct that would posit a series of architectural pieces that would throw shadows upon other pieces and present the occupants with a series of extant *and* implicit foci. The plan presents these all as equals.

In showing the sketch, the ink drawing and then the coloured drawing together, we can access the project in different ways. They raise the inevitable question as to the 'essential' moment of a work. If the pencilled plan is the first registration of the idea, it has authorship over the rest. Yet in parts it is

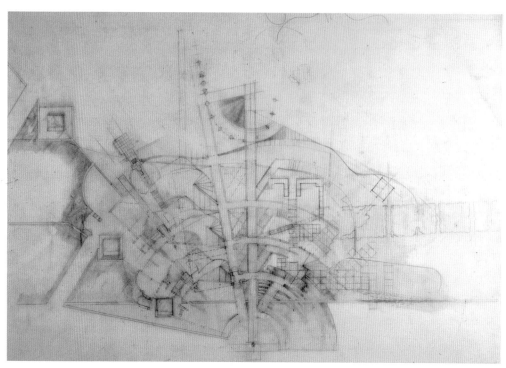

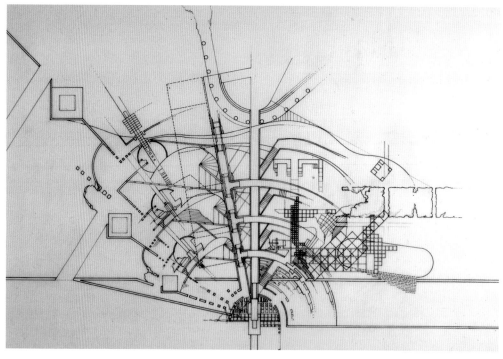

Christine Hawley, Shadow House, 1980. Pencil and tracing paper, 48 x 65.5 cm. Deutsches Architekturmuseum Collection, Frankfurt/Main.

indistinct and the ink drawing not only discriminates and refines, but also defines, Hawley's intention (which I seem to remember, being there from the first), was to make the coloured drawing the definitive one. It is able to codify some of the parts: to imply water, solidity, the essential, the incidental and that which fades away.

The three drawings sit together in the Deutsches Architekturmuseum in Frankfurt and naturally it is the coloured version that is seen in publications. No doubt from time to time a researcher looks at the other two versions. Yet neither of them is a freehand 'sketch'. They are a continuous part of a single process. The image of the scheme is this romantic, semicircular composition. It says enough about the combination of parts, enough about the physiognomy of the architecture. Yet there is a popular view that a sketch is the legitimate first statement and that a 'worked' drawing gains in a certain professional sense and loses the delightful innocence of the sketch. It is one of those myths. The continuous lap-over set is just as heroic in its own way.

Christine Hawley, Shadow House, 1980. Ink on tracing paper, 71.2 x 98 cm. Deutsches Architekturmuseum Collection, Frankfurt/Main.

Christine Hawley, Shadow House, 1980. Ink, airbrush, watercolour and pencil on cardboard. Deutsches Architekturmuseum Collection, Frankfurt/Main.

Peter Cook, Sleek (part of
Arcadia project), 1977. Ink and
airbrushed coloured inks, 70
x 70 cm. (Line drawing made
in 1966 and previously part of
Sponge project.) Deutsches
architecturmuseum Collection,
Frankfurt/Main.

Capturing spontaneity is not the same thing as spontaneity itself. In my Sleek (1977) drawing I am fixing down an idea that took about half a minute to think of: namely, the creation of an entirely artificial and luxuriant urban building. Inevitably it must be made from glass or plastic. It must eschew the natural. No timber or stone here, no paint, no little screw points or unnecessary joints – the dream of positive artificiality. Allowing only the occasional deliberate blemish of the bubble outbursts – in the tradition of the planted 'beauty spot' on the face of the 18th-century coquette – draws attention to the perfection of the rest of the surface. A small plantation is also present – threatening the artificial, but nonetheless subsumed by it.

Such a programme – of purely Expressionist notions – was there almost in a flash, probably the by-product of discussions in seminars or whatever. The task was just to draw it, no further thinking being necessary. The line drawing took a few hours: not difficult if well controlled by my kit of compasses and straight-edges. But the colouring was a joy only in the anticipation. We must remember that this was in the days before Photoshop, and thus involved many sessions of masking and cutting in order for the airbrushing process to occur. It had to incorporate many moments of touching up to correct the several imperfections of the masking. As with the coquette's face, this piece of sophistication demanded the deceit of the make-up artist.

It has continued to amuse me that this piece has been one of the most often published of my own drawings, particularly as a cover picture during the late 1980s and the 1990s. Others of my pieces interest me more, have more to say about architecture, have cute aspects for a fellow connoisseur, or myself: but Sleek looks the part.

Presumably it has image quality.

5
Drawing and Composition

The prediction of architecture forms the central theme of this book. The creation of that architecture depends upon a combination of describable moves based on generally recognised values, but it can also be the result of much less describable moves that stem from notions of balance, sequence, elegance, the confrontation of parts and the harnessing of forces, all of which add up to the art of composition.

For many reasons – some economic, some political, some ethical – this particular art has dropped out of architectural discussion. Composition is looked upon by some as an arcane, even indulgent, pursuit that brings architecture back to the status of a wilful art form, and it is even seen as being contrary to the notions of 'honesty' or 'fitness for purpose' that underscored much of the reasoning used to authenticate 20th-century buildings. Yet if we prise away these objections and evaluate the best work (of any mannerism) and try to analyse its strengths in contrast with lesser work of the same genre, we soon enter the territories of balance, sequence and the rest that make up a value system. Stepping outside architecture to the areas of music, literature and drama – but also to psychology and military strategy – we can sense a general system at work, whereby the forces of the work are sequenced, weighed up against each other, released into the sequences at various moments and, inevitably, edited in such a way that the result is either charming, coercive, dramatic, intentionally surprising or made up of contrasted sequences.

Paul Bigot, A Thermal Bathing
Establishment and Casino, 1900.
Plan and elevation.

There are particular stages in the process of design when the parts are
beginning to be understood, but still lie in a series of uncomfortable
juxtapositions demanding a distanced view of them to be taken. Rarely a
single step, the process of composition has on the one hand the frustration
that there may not be a 'correct' assemblage of elements, but on the other
hand it introduces the delight of creating conditions that are more than just
the sum of their parts. It could be that the long, slow return to the valuation
of composition required the distance of time that we now have between
ourselves and the late 19th century. During that period, the École des Beaux-
Arts in Paris was the acknowledged leader of architectural values by way of
the sophistication with which it evoked procedures of sequence, balance or

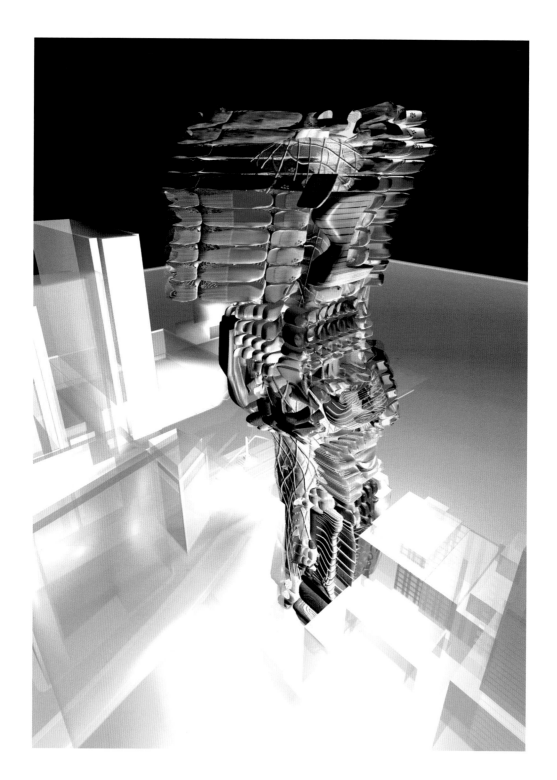

discrimination (for example, see Paul Bigot's Thermal Bathing Establishment and Casino, 1900). The school combined the sophistry of trickery and seduction with the art of making the ordinary seem special. That this could encompass varying reinterpretations of Classicism as well as absorb much of the Romantic palette rendered it a powerful force.

The rhetorical utterances of Modernism have very often seemed to contain a thinly veiled critique of the whole Beaux-Arts syndrome that bordered on the shrill. Yet it soon became obvious that simply aiming for a single, abstracted language of walls had limitations, just as the simple throwing down of 'working parts' upon a site realised little from its potential. Composition manqué crept in and the pre-eminent role of the drawing can be recognised as its most accessible medium.

The drawing can summon up forces that have been kept on the sidelines, it can celebrate the unheroic, it can creatively distort, it can divide and rule, but most of all it can suddenly decide to totally reinvent – taking the known parts and giving them newly discovered roles. It is not always best for drawings to be accurate: better sometimes for them to insert moments of a dream or a diversion into the otherwise commonplace procedure of describing and organising.

At this point I accede to a temptation by invoking one of the most magical of computer-generated drawings to celebrate the fact that the art of composition has returned to full strength.

Composition Revived

The ResiRise Skyscraper project, exhibited by New York-based architects Sulan Kolatan and William MacDonald (KOL/MAC LLC) in the US Pavilion at the 2004 Venice Architecture Biennale, takes full advantage of the form that can be summoned by the creative coercion and tracking that comes out of the digitalised process. Some of the parts of this tower structure seem to have an inevitability about them, stemming maybe from a zone on the site or from the setting of a sequence of repetition. Yet the subtlety of the growth elasticises the state of inevitability so that one realises that the sequence has metamorphosed. Against such a sequence there rises another sequence that reserves the right to outcrop and surprise at another pace, with another characteristic of bulbousness with insidious counter-growths creeping along meanwhile.

Sulan Kolatan and William MacDonald (KOL/MAC LLC), ResiRise Skyscraper, New York, US, 1999. Aerial perspective view from the south-east towards Central Park: digitally rendered image file (using Autodesk Maya software).

Those of us who have been inspired by the notion of waywardness and metamorphosis, of less-than-orthogonal forms, warping, collaging or multi-paced syncopation in the extrapolation of a building have found such things hard to draw with pencils, pens and templates. Possible to imagine, but frustrating to perform. Now they can be depicted and, of course, built.

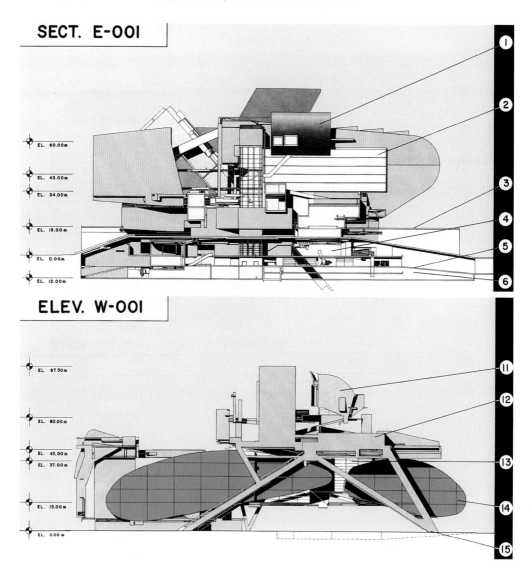

Within the process of such a project lies the inspirational aspect of digital architecture whereby the setting of instigators and parameters sets up a process of growth that needs only to be tweaked by the designer. This is a partisan claim, yet it soon becomes obvious that the result of such a process can range (as it always has) from the banal, the predictable, past the delightful, the quizzical and the unpleasant. In other words, compositional control is of the essence. Whether the direct analogy is via predictive steps, trial and error or revision and editing, the lack of a pencil does not prevent this being a process of drawing.

ResiRise is composed in such a way that it states the state of speculation for a building at which we comprehend it and appreciate its nuances. In such a way, it has made us a drawing of that building.

The two elevations for the Tokyo International Forum competition of 1989 identify both the potential of the elevation as a summary statement and the formidable talent of the LA architect and 'machine architecture' protagonist Neil Denari. More than almost anyone else, Denari can turn a line or cut into a surface with a dexterity of placement that is uncanny. That these are flat drawings, rendered mostly in a single weight of line, economical with colour and deliberately untextured, prepares us for the few dramatic moments when uncompromising black shadows remind us of the three-dimensionality of the thing.

Another surprise lies in the heroic range of scale that is represented. Denari is able to be both gigantean (just look at those Goliath legs that straddle the green volumes) and finicky (just pick your way among the balconies and ramps of the upper drawing). In earlier works, such as that for the Tower of London, he had already displayed his penchant for the combination of mechanised elements with large, bulk areas of containment. In the Tokyo project, he seems to effortlessly present us with combinations of the reasonable: stripes of serviceable floors, one upon the other, intriguing series of cuts into the taller elements, and then a series of incidental built parts that sneak past, peek out, dangle down. That one can describe these flat drawings with such a dramatic scenario tells of the inventiveness of the piece.

In 2&1/2D (twoandahalf dimensionality) (2006), a drawing by Italian London-based architect Marjan Colletti, there is an extension to the act of composition that seems to run beyond those we have already identified: instead of merely tweaking or cutting into surfaces, he chooses to virtually

Marjan Colletti, 2&1/2D
(twoandahalf dimensionality)
#22: Beyond surfaces and blobs,
2006. Digital print.

'grow' the construct before our very eyes. There are outpourings that are quasi-landscape, but never actual landscape. There are components that have a regularity and commonality – yet are by no means facsimiles of each other. And there are components that appear to be hybrids or products of each other: shells that do not so much burst but transfigure in the process of exploding out. At this point in the observation, one becomes both suspicious and inspired by the possibility that the compositional act and the compositional process are, in this case, an analogous process by which the computer is directed and encouraged in this creation.

The Champion of the Axonometric

As an instrument for summarising the compositional act, the axonometric remains a fast and reliable model. Bypassed now by the ability of the computer program to twist, turn, re-present and re-present three-dimensional information, it had a solid, matter-of-factness that suited its hero, James Stirling, perfectly. Notably in the period of the 1960s to the 1990s, this form of projection became very popular among architects. You simply took a plan and drew up from it at a consistent angle (or angled the plan underneath the tracing paper to suit the drawing upwards of vertical lines). Stirling relished his inventiveness with strong, sometimes toy-like elements, needing few variations of surface beyond solid and glazed, depending upon the bold turning of 90 or 45 degrees in the process.

His drawing for the History Faculty Building of the University of Cambridge (1963–67) sets the figure out, and its main compositional moves are extant. The 'L' of the holding 'wall' permits the great glasshouse to tumble within: the rest is nuance. Famed among his students and associates for making endless small drawings that concentrated on the composition of the main parts of a project, it seems as if the published axonometrics such as this one were merely a stylised extension of such jottings.

Placing the parts in a clear way is one of the fundamentals of composition, yet it can so often be subsumed beneath other tantalising aspects of a project. In some cases, the 'game' can even be that of 'hunt the parts' so that a seeming homogeneity or scrambling of hierarchies is deliberately set up in order to deny the obviousness of the basic composition. Not so with the late New York architect and educator John Hejduk's isometric for the Wall House 2 (AE Bye House) project of 1973.

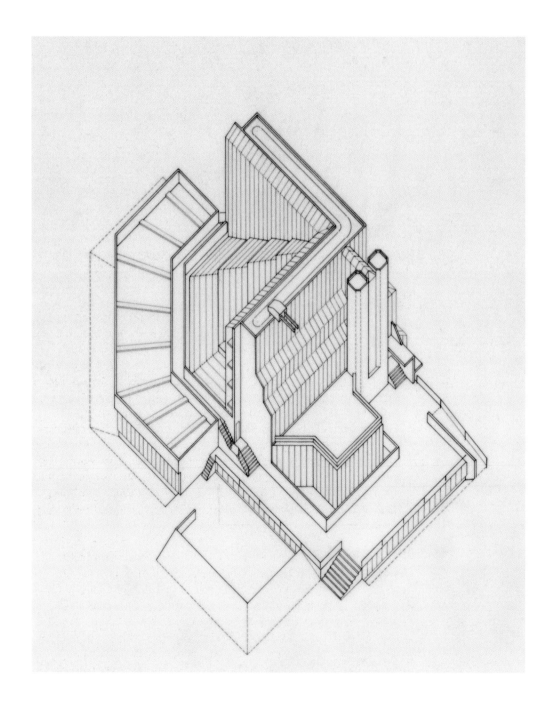

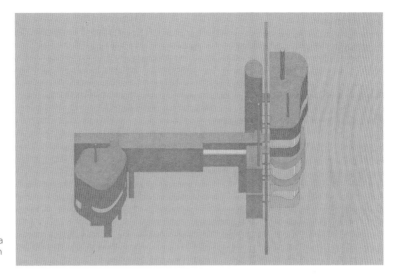

John Hejduk, Wall House 2
(AE Bye House), Ridgefield,
Connecticut, US, 1973–6.
Isometric (1973): crayon on sepia
diazotype, 71 x 102 cm. Museum
of Modern Art, New York.

At this stage of his work, the reference to a Corbusian inspiration is clear
in the mannerism of the five elements that I will describe as 'cabins'. The
wall that gives its name to the project – and is therefore assumed to be
its focus – is unusually long, but the key compositional activity is actually
that of attachment. Giving each cabin a distinctive colour and a particular
shape, Hejduk clarifies the act. Each is detached from the basic 'T' armature,
itself depicted in neutral grey. The choice of coloured pencil applied in two
pressures – soft and full on – gives the drawing a mandate in two categories
at once. First, it is simple and colour coded, so it can be used as an analytical
diagram, but the two weights of colour add three-dimensional information
that tells us more about the form than would a simple, all-over colour code.
The contrast of the neutral grey (actually using two different hues of grey,
one of them in two weights), allows the analytical distinction of the building
to be made.

Further observation reveals Hejduk's skill and confidence in such details
as his recourse to a pale-blue strip window (but no colouring of the other
windows), plus his choice of column colouration: the grey column is not so
much an adjunct to the box of building, but part of it. The red column is
similarly part of the cabin tower.

James Stirling, History
Faculty Building, University
of Cambridge, UK, 1963–7.
Axonometric, graphite and
ink on translucent paper,
34.1 x 27.8 cm.

In pedantically stripping down such a beautifully modest drawing I wish
to draw special attention to the issue of motive, category, definition and

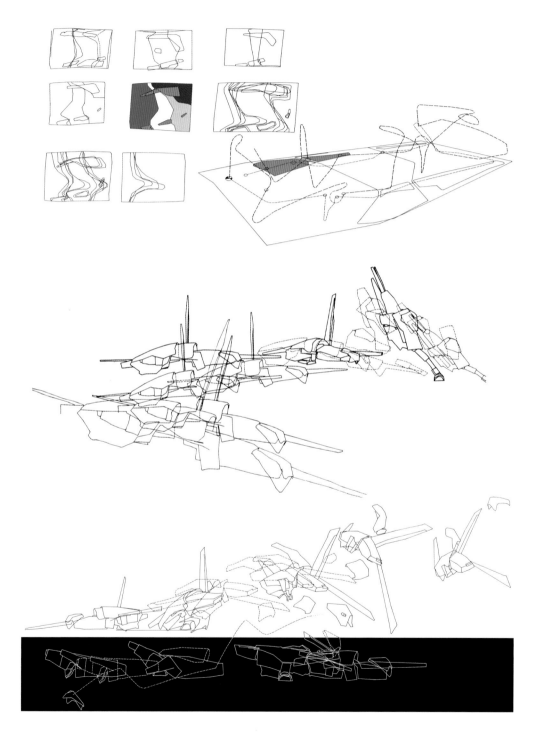

CJ Lim, Guest House, Japan, 1995. Pen and ink on film with acrylic paint.

aesthetic at the same time. Its simplicity is not the result of a reductive or minimalist approach: quite the contrary. The piece is full of nuance and taste as well as definition. Hejduk was a brilliant pedagogue who often set compositional-procedural exercises for his students and who, via his friend, painter and architectural theorist Robert Slutzky, had a close knowledge of the procedures of Josef Albers and others connected to Purism.

CJ Lim is another pedagogue who has developed his range and skills of designing and drawing to fantastic lengths – always two steps ahead of his students and always benefiting from the discipline of spelling out the process of compositional design through drawing. At the same time, we shall see here and in other chapters Lim's recourse to a series of techniques that nag at the essence of a piece – often involving dynamic as applied to placement. Thus we see objects dissected, gyrated, tracked across space and seen in

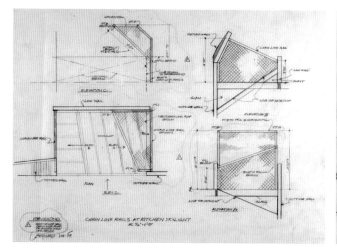
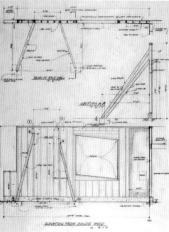

Frank Gehry, Gehry Residence, Santa Monica, California, US, 1978. Pencil and coloured pencil on tracing paper.

different contexts, yet in the process questioned and identified as much for their cultural ambiguity as for their formal measure.

Who is the Audience?

Discussing the work of such an exciting architect as Frank Gehry is an irresistible temptation if we are concerned with the history of composition, but I deliberately chose to approach it from a modest example of drawing that is surely revealing. The drawings for his own house in Santa Monica, which was built in 1978, are straightforward working drawings made in pencil. They use nothing more than the usual conventions of a standard weight of line nearly all of the time – intensified only when something is seen in section. There are dimension lines and squiggled arrow paths to distinguish such lines from those for the built pieces. Colour is used only once – for the door.

Yet the eccentricity of the house and the deftness of its original composition are revealed. You do not have to use elaborate drawing to make such a statement. Even the building technique itself is a twisted version of the normal, so the commonplace nature of the whole process throws the issue simply back to that of wit. The extraordinary iconic quality of the house that has drawn hundreds of thousands of observers and sneak photographers to it since 1980 had to be communicated to normal, jobbing craftsmen. Raising now, the issue of 'audience'.

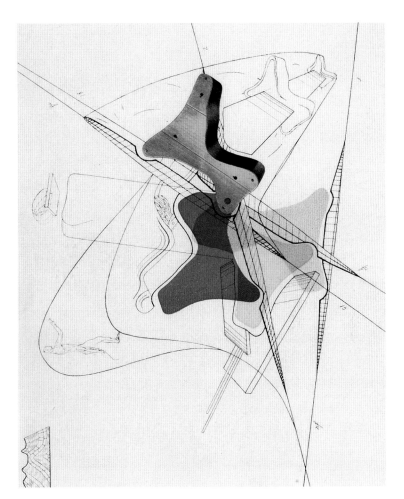

Frederick Kiesler, Study for the Different Functions of the 'Correalist Instrument', New York, US, 1943. Montage with eyelet, ink and tempera on cardboard.

Does a drawing assume its degree of rhetoric according to its presumed audience? No rhetoric at all for the working drawing. A little more for the proposal made for fellow professionals. A little more still for the proposal made for a lay committee. Whizz-bang for the newspaper. Further on, and the computerised fly-through takes over. Yet galleries and collectors hanker after the presumed 'authenticity' of the working drawing or the generic scribble, searching for clues as to the moment of creativity.

The drawings by the Austro-American architect Frederick Kiesler, who became associated with the Surrealists after he emigrated to the US in the 1920s, are far more difficult to assess than almost anyone else's. They have very little attraction as graphics and are often difficult to follow. As propositions, however, they can be extraordinary; as combinations of various differing criteria or indications of unlikely objects in unlikely combinations they must surely be read in the same manner as Marcel Duchamp's Large

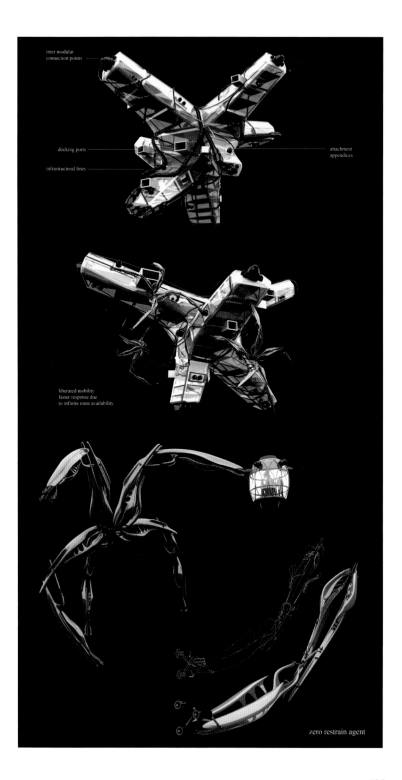

inter modular
connection points

docking ports

infrastructural lines

attachment
appendices

liberated mobility
faster response due
to infinite route availability

zero restrain agent

Glass. Though a maker of objects, Kiesler's range and imagination ran far further than that of his commissions and needed, perhaps, the ability (that a drawing has) to jump scale, context or criteria – unlike a made object.

Therefore the Study for the Different Functions of the 'Correalist Instrument' (1943) – a typical piece – makes considerable demands upon the viewer. Do not be deceived by the curvy stylisation, devised, perhaps, more for the reminder of the idea of 'instrument' and the device of the guitar-like shaping of the central, referential element. But from then on we have to keep our eyes out for little quotes and twists. A figure here, a constructible object there, a possibly operational device somewhere else. Architectural overtones to the whole: is it a building, an interior, an assemblage? Is it using the idea of musical instrument as an analogy, or should we treat it as a direct reference? The contrast of the folded planes to the straight plates – is this 'architecture' again? The fretted fins – what are they? Such a drawing asks all these questions of us, but perhaps suggests an overriding answer in telling us that architectural exploration as well as its methods of composition need, from time to time, to be explored through the confrontation of the unlike with the unlike and the irregular with the irregular. Drawing has the potential to extend the instigation and the language.

Compositional Hybrids and the Collage Drawing

Edward McIntosh, Alternatives to High-Rise Circulation, New York, US, 2006. Digital modelling/collage, 5400 x 10,800 pixels 300 dpi.

In his Alternatives to High-Rise Circulation (2006), Columbia University graduate Edward McIntosh uses today's techniques of assemblage to create what he calls a 'scattered tower' that attempts to dispense with vertical circulation and a notion of friction attachment. The composition of the parts is always under threat of slippage or reconfiguration, but then the whole thing is a hybrid asking itself whether it is made up of a series of transportation devices or architectural elements.

The choice of drawing type is intriguing, for once again it is a hybrid. With the computer you can equally easily create a linear or a quasi-solid image. You can combine into it details, surfaces, mannerisms from anywhere, creating ghosts, toys, diagrams or pictures of the most uncanny realism. McIntosh chooses a currently preferred combination of diagram and shiny neo-reality.

The more architectonic parts are rendered in grey and have some captions. The distinction of the neo-vehicular (or is it aquatic?) parts is that they are 'gilded' – or at least given a certain patina of glamour. The metallic implication of them is probably deliberate (even though the rest may well also be made of metal), and the two series are further distinguished by an implication of modularity to the grey parts (architecture), but sexy muscularity for the twisting attachments. Intriguingly, there is a white line diagram there also for reference.

I dwell upon this combination of freedom and studied nonchalance of the creative idea and almost traditional symbolism of the rendering, as if to bend towards the world of the advertising brochure and its normality in dealing with an abnormal proposition. Underlying the mannerism of many good computer drawings may be a very deliberate wish for them not to look technical or abstracted, or made up of line configurations – as did the old, wrist-movement-based drawings. After all, the computer can get it to look *very* real – and then we can step back from this near-reality any number of steps we care to?

Peter Cook, Oslo East, Norway, 2005. Elevation/section: ink, gouache, watercolour and coloured pencil, 210 x 35 cm.

Peter Cook, Oslo East, Norway, 2005. Cartoon commentary: reversed print, photocopies, photography, watercolour as collage.

I continue myself with my traditional system of drawing in ink and then colouring prints. I start laying out a series of buildings along a line cut through a plan and admit that in my project for the railyards behind Oslo main station, 2005, I worked from an approximate, or 'sketch', plan only. The section-elevation drawing makes more investigations (and certainly makes more detailed suggestions) than the plan. Immediately after this exercise I deliberately made the lower collage drawing with selected pieces of detail plan here and there.

As important as these are the texts and collaged-in items. They combine references to other, earlier projects – particularly a small coloured plan from an earlier run at the same idea as here, for a canal running inside a covered arcade – and to concurrent projects, such as the Vallecas housing for Madrid (2007). The Oslo housing to the right of the drawing, though different in both profile and fenestration, has certain organisational similarities. The relative speed at which it was drawn stems from the day-to-

day awareness of the minutiae of social housing rules. Another day-to-day involvement certainly comes from my consultancy at HOK Sport where I am regularly called upon to comment on the architectural qualities of stadiums: so this little one for eastern Oslo has a certain relaxedness about it that it would not have otherwise.

Incorporating such dramatic elements as a stadium, an island-based office tower or lines of railway observing (both consciously and subconsciously) the apparatus of the 'North Sea Syndrome', which is one of my favourite sets of inspiration, becomes partly homogenised by the common application of watercolour and the occasional application of coloured pencil or gouache. In compositional terms, there is a certain sideways consciousness that leads you to establish 'key' references such as the office tower, and key mannerisms such as the similarity of construction of the bridge and the water-arcade roof. After this comes a more subtle attempt to instigate a gradual change of mannerism from left to right, which is from seaward to landward for the housing. The role of superimposed vegetation is critical and the drawing acts as a test bed for ideas of internal planting, external swathes of planting and the vegetation of public spaces. Section drawings enabled one to show the necessary tucking and folding of vegetation among the apertures of the perforated deck that lies above the railway tracks.

Much of this is talked about in the Oslo collage drawing.

In my earlier work during the Archigram period – Way Out West–Berlin, 1988 (see Chapter 2), Sponge City, 1975 (see Chapter 3) and Veg House, 1996–2001 (see Chapter 8) for instance – the commentary was limited or presented in short pieces of text. The collage drawing here should be read as a kind of 'parallel text' as used in biblical translations or even some form of guide-sheet. To what extent it has its own aesthetic I am not sure, nor to what extent it can stand alone as a drawing in its own right.

It is clear that the composing of a drawing for its own sake has dangers: to coerce an architectural project 'for the picture' contains a certain cynicism. It is parallel, however, to the established habit of putting all the fancy architecture on the street side and letting the back just come as it may. Yet the use of the drawing in assembling the project: this surely is a wonderful experience.

Drawing with Expression and Atmosphere

In the late 20th century a new phenomenon emerged that took a number of architects by surprise: the art public (or at least, a segment of it) was becoming interested in architectural drawings. Though acknowledged as a component of the old Academy system, working architects had held to their known territory and assumed that 'art' only came in if necessary for 'presentation'. Paradoxically many had been encouraged into the profession because they could draw well, yet firmly discouraged from becoming 'artists' by their families. This therefore created a situation where people of imagination have had that instinct fettered and redirected towards a procedural world in which imagination is considered suspect. If we track the careers of many of the contributors to this book, we will find that they include many 'academics' – a loose term that encompasses creative architects who spend a lot of time teaching. Others will come under the category of 'polemicists' – which covers some major architects who, in the early stages of their careers, made extreme statements and often extreme drawings to accompany those statements. Others find ways in which they can recall those first murmurings of fierce imagination and erupt into visual rhetoric at key moments, knowing that somewhere in the background the necessarily prosaic working drawings can follow through.

The 'morality of the ordinary' has already been alluded to, but even if one subscribed to it (which I certainly do not), there would be a large question mark hanging over the business of 'condition'.

We can state something as an inventory, as an arrangement of parts, as a layout, as a timetable. We can show the distinct and correct position of the arrangement. We can now very easily depict this arrangement from every conceivable viewpoint. Yet something is missing. What is it like? How might it feel to be there? Is it bland, fresh, lively, shiny, wispy, heavy, gloomy or spooky? In making an effort to answer such questions we have to communicate. In the process, too, we may well coerce those same mute 'arrangements' of parts into having character. We may start to consider such character at the outset. In this sense, the drawing itself becomes intrinsically predictive; there is an uncut loop of memory, observation and creativity in which condition is the pre-eminent force.

The word 'expression' has tricky connotations in the architectural world, largely through its connotation with Expressionism itself. In art and architecture it centres on certain German work of the early 20th century, which is characterised by an enormous verve and dynamic. In this chapter we will pass through pieces by Lebbeus Woods, Hermann Finsterlin, Hugh Ferriss and Luke Chandresinghe, all of which possess such dynamic. Yet none of them (with the arguable exception of Finsterlin) comes into the historic category of Expressionism. It is atmosphere and dynamic, as much as form and detail, that hold our attention in work that sits outside our own period or culture. Is it that 'arrangement' is for the professionals and the rest is for contemplation? Beyond this lies an awkward question as to the need for intellectual stimulation. Art collectors are drawn to architectural drawings that are highly (or apparently) technical and one wonders whether this is in order to contemplate the mystery of the unknown – which one might describe as the 'Dead Sea Scroll' syndrome – or to avoid the criticism that architects, when being expressive, are just 'bad artists'.

The Power of the Depictive Image

The subject matter, the choice of method and the architectural resource all combine to deflect such criticism in a work such as The Hanging Cemetery of Baghdad (2005) by Nannette Jackowski and Ricardo de Ostos of London-based practice NaJa and deOstos. The conception of the piece is the result of endless conversation between the joint artists who, in paralleling a long series of drawings with a powerful text, are able to produce a narrative piece. There is a political and critical rhetoric involved, there are complex overlays of German and Brazilian-Venezuelan background developed against an English

NaJa and deOstos, The Hanging
Cemetery of Baghdad, 2005.
3-D model rendering.

culture, with the place and events detached by distance and circumstance,
and there is the overlay of graphic techniques and degrees of 'reality'.

The resultant drawing has all of these layers lying within it. Furthermore, it
is by architects who are also teaching relatively young, involving with it a
sense of 'declaration' in which they lay out their stall: of the generation that
is already comfortable with the computer but also highly articulate in hand
drawing. One can, of course, just take a look at the imagery and conclude
from its impact. Yet here we are necessarily unravelling and predicting the
successful continuation of the 'depictive' drawing.

Equally depictive and now historically acknowledged lies *The Peak: Blue
Slabs* painting of The Peak Club, Hong Kong, by Zaha Hadid of 1982–3 (see
Chapter 3). This apocryphal view of the territory that would surround her
unrealised competition win suggests a Hong Kong Island that is of itself, yet
more than itself. Hadid captured the staccato verticality of the place with its
'knives cutting through the site'. In its particular form of abstraction it recalls
her considerable knowledge of Russian Suprematism. It prepares the observer
for the power of the Peak building itself – which is predominantly made up
of swirling horizontals. In its avoidance of the tiresome inconsistencies and
details of the aerial photograph or the realistic perspective, it has the strength
and the arrogance to call us to order and insist that we recognise the values
inherent in the project itself.

Since 1980, it could be said that the architectural world has been consistently challenged by the imagery of two architects (who happen to be close friends) who have little fear and immense resource of originality. Thus in jumping from the abstraction of the Hadid painting to the detail and patina of drawings by the American visionary architect Lebbeus Woods, I am not in any way relaxing the pressure. Rather I am celebrating this sense of power, which in Woods' case stems from a background of engineering studies and building, before the moment when the sheer creativity of his renderings for commercial architects focused so much that they outshone the buildings themselves. By this time anyway, progression of themes from small follies, through aerial cities and on to 'commentary' projects in which cities known and circumstances experienced (Berlin in the 1990s and Sarajevo during the Civil War) made Woods' work both ecstatic through its presence and challenging through its stance. Jackowski and de Ostos are surely the children of his method.

In the Berlin Free Zone (1990) he is depicting a hybrid condition that allows organised, folded parts to spawn intriguing tentacles that appear to both

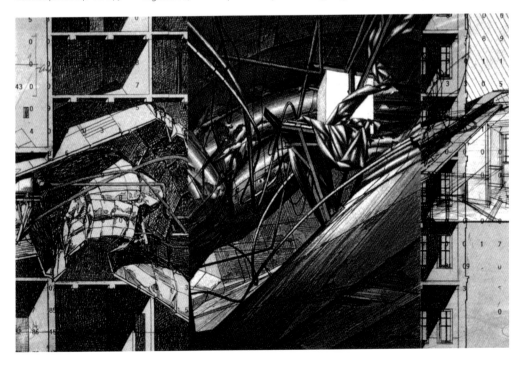

twirl and drift. This has the effect of both tantalising us into wondering what additional forces are at work to challenge or feed the vessel itself while at the same time accentuating the notion of movement and speed. Unlike the ambiguity of McIntosh's composition in Chapter 5, the vehicular and tectonic parts are nearly of one family, but only just.

It is undoubtedly the task of such a drawing to push the language and context of architecture forward. It also has an atmospheric quality that challenges us – nearly real, and yet … maybe surreal?

In such a drawing there is a combination of straightforward architectural referencing within which the faint quotation of plan is then superimposed by a more insistent (but equally commonplace) set-up of a section – with just enough revelation of the ordinariness of the windows in elevation and a certain grimness of the interior space to be given by the shadows. Into this leaps the Woods object. Colour suddenly announces a strange set of

Peter Wilson, Water House, Shinkenchiku Residential Design Competition, Tokyo, 1976. Black pencil on tracing paper with coloured accents on A3 paper.

twirling wraps and shattering planes; once again there are those tantalising strings or tubes and shards of a material that is certainly freer than that of the surrounding building.

All of this is handled within a rich consistency of pencil technique that is sparing of its colour palette. Like John Hejduk's Wall House 2 (1973), featured in Chapter 5, it allows a knowing break in the rules, so that the black-and-white patch tolerates red and green tubes. The implication here is surely to do with focus. There is a variable insistence on the viewer to look – and then look again.

We shall examine Woods' work later on in discussing the back-and-forth between drawing and experienced three-dimensionality.

The Calm and the Slamming

So far as establishing a detachment from reality into a possible, but unlikely, condition (let us call it a reverie), the Water House (1976) by the Australian-born Peter Wilson of German-based practice Bolles + Wilson remains a key work. As with Woods, the deftness of the drawn lines themselves are there to seduce. Water is notoriously difficult to depict and here it is central to the project. It seems to spurt out with a necessary inevitability. It is, after all, a Romantic concept, demanding a simplicity from the architecture, suggesting a prerequisite calmness of context – all of which Wilson is able to convey in a restricted medium.

Deliberately, I follow the calmness of the Water House with an (only just) architectonic slammer of a project. Will Alsop and Tim Thornton's Museum at Glenwood Powerhouse, Yonkers, New York (2006) explodes into a virtual context of its own around the 'house' element. As abstracted in its own way as Hadid's Peak, it has cartooned splodges of 'tree', 'bush' and 'cloud' plus some mysterious 'rings' – what do they depict? There is a knowing scatter that falls upon the box of the house itself and must become its surface treatment. Yet the functioning segment of the building has just enough depiction to make itself felt in Alsop's painting. Much of his built work is first investigated through such paintings, which are in some ways influenced by those of his friend, artist Bruce McLean. Indeed, there are now a number of buildings by him in England, France and Canada that have made the creative leap from such a scattering of confrontational icons as these to the actual building.

Alsop Architects, One of a series
of computer-generated colour
options for The Sharp Centre,
Ontario College of Art & Design,
Toronto, Canada, 2001.

Will Alsop and Tim Thornton, Museum at Glenwood Powerhouse, Yonkers, New York, US. Charcoal, paint and mirror on paper, 2006.

As we found in Cedric Price's work, the choice of apparently simple devices is deliberate and maintains the clarity of intention. In the more formal renderings of Alsop's work, the controlled zaniness of legs and hues and exotic fragments is never polite and serves as developmental drawing. The Powerhouse leaves us still wondering what the actual building will look like in terms of materiality, finesse, precise positioning of parts, but leaves us in no doubt about the thrust of the idea. However, in his Sharp Centre for the Ontario College of Art & Design in Toronto (2001), we have no doubt about such things, but are itching to know just how it came about. One could, of course, apply such enquiry to any project. But Alsop's verve, daring and confrontation invite the question, and it is consummately (though for some, frighteningly) answered by the large paintings. An argument for the presentation of serial drawings exposed to the public with the motives and process spelled out?

If we look further back to a point in the development of Modernism when the first Purist and Constructivist statements had been made, but with a range and application that was still open to discovery, there emerged from Russia a 'paper' architect of such graphic boldness that both the monochrome and the narrowness of range of many of his peers was challenged. Iakov Chernikov's key work was his *Architectural Fantasies:*

Iakov Chernikhov, Architectural
Fantasy, 1928. Ink and gouache
on paper, 31.2 x 25.1 cm. Published
as Composition 75 in the book
*Architectural Fantasies: 101
Compositions* (Leningrad, 1933).

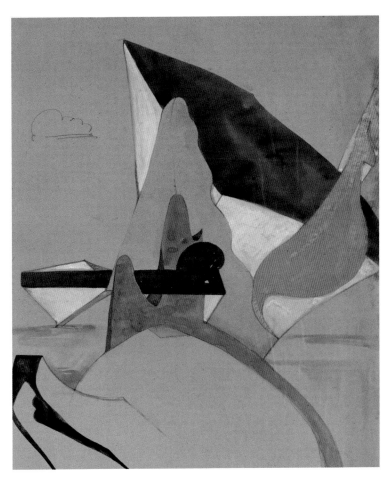

Hermann Finsterlin, Architektur, 1970. Copy reworked with pencil and coloured pencil on cardboard.

Hermann Finsterlin, Architektur, 1920. Pencil, watercolour on paper and cardboard, 50.3 x 38.3 cm. Deutsches Architekturmuseum Collection, Frankfurt/Main.

101 Compositions (published in 1933), which centred on complexes that had an 'industrial' overtone. Massive chunks of building are juxtaposed against frames of megastructural girth, cylindrical objects are posed against bands of mesh or (implicit) window. The exuberance – but at the same time the consistency of expression – gave them a certain quality that was beyond architecture.

Dismissed by some at the time as too 'graphic', the *Fantasies* have outlasted many of the other Russian visions through their clarity, their completeness, and their surefooted attitude towards the presence of the object. An irresistible mass of blue or a leaping band of red – such attack is hard to withstand.

Some 12 years before, the German Expressionist architect, painter and poet Hermann Finsterlin had presented an equally colourful shock to the system of architectural investigation. His Architektur of 1920 is far less well known than most of his work, but its mysteriousness renders it tantalisingly radical. After all, the encompassing forms were not solids, but more like 'drapes', and they drifted here and there. Their patchily applied watercolour fails to dissuade their provocation. As with the Frederick Kiesler drawing in Chapter 5, there is the suggestion of arrangement, the occasional suggestion of solidity, with planes establishing a territory and then letting it go by refusing to draw more lines that might relate it all to a system. Yet there is a condition of interlock and just a hint that this might all be stemming from – or outcropping from – another and larger body. Only now do I realise that it is such work that has sat in my subconscious when working on a building like the Kunsthaus Graz – realising that the business of folding in and outcropping is a necessary celebration of the power of the more major elements.

A very much later coloured-pencil drawing by Finsterlin discloses many of the hinted-at conditions of the watercolour. Bulbous conditions are complete. Curved surfaces sit as 'plates' or 'roofs'. Scoops of space are differentiated and imply surface treatment as would be appropriate to sheltered sideways-on conditions. The composition is exciting and still provocative, but the follow-through is well mannered. As with the two Alsop drawings, we can see the jump from the implicit to the explicit. Apart from the salutary thought that his work anticipates the explorations of Kolatan and MacDonald or Díaz Alonso, one continues to search the world of drawings to elucidate those magic moments wherein the exploration of architecture is discovering new states of language and expression.

Peter Cook, Hulk (deliberately incomplete carcass for a future apartment building), Real City project, Frankfurt/Offenbach, Germany, 1987. Ink and watercolour.

My own Real City (1987) project, an urban proposal for linking Frankfurt with Offenbach, involved the idea of half-built structures that could later be infilled by either temporary structures or 'proper' architecture. The perspective drawing Hulk formed part of a series – the rest of which dealt with completed buildings. In some ways it dramatised the brooding, mysterious quality that you sometimes see when passing by an uncompleted framed building in the twilight. The intention was that the over-scaled mass could be constructed from a mixture of concrete and junk materials, and the cracks and imperfect edges were meant to be symbolic of this. Yet the whole is rendered in a yellow tone – itself provocative? Beckoning the squatters or the developers to come and do something with it. An overtone of historic relic – of forgotten city as well as real city – is implicated.

The Observer's Culture

At this point, one can deliberately pull back towards a simple housing proposal for Frankfurt, the Siedlung Riederwald (Riederwald housing estate), from the 1920s and the team of Ernst May, H Boehm, E + O Fucker and F Thyriot. The drawing is deadpan. The statement of expression

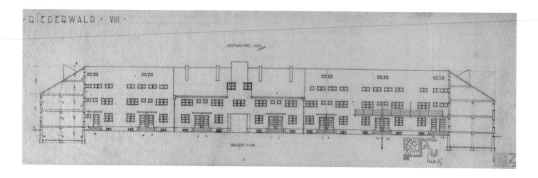

or atmosphere is reduced right down to the mere placement of floors, windows and doors. To the initiate, the nature of those windows and doors and the mullion and transom lines, as well as the realisation that the roof direction reverses between the centre of the block and its ends, give sufficient clues as to the likely atmosphere of the place. To the uninitiated, it may remain a rather dull old line drawing. To a certain partisan group of architects, this in itself will be a virtue.

So at this point we have to deal with the question of the observer and the observer's culture. Within the world of architecture, and if you are prepared to bother, the simple line drawing is enough. If you wish to be stimulated, as a fellow architect, the exploded painting of the Alsop painting is a provocation, or at least a wake-up call. Yet we always hope that architecture and its development within the broader culture is no mere coterie pursuit. The maker of the drawing must choose the territory, but must also choose that state of evolution of the project at which it is useful (or provocative) to expose the game.

In order to promote a great exhibition and to tantalise a resourceful, but polite, public, the Swedish Neoclassicist Gunnar Asplund had the need to make jolly, exciting drawings of an event that, indeed, became apocryphal. It can now be seen that the Stockholm Exhibition of 1930 was a key overlap between the rhetoric of the new Soviet architecture of the 1920s and 1930s and the more mildly socialist world of Scandinavia and the West. There was still an essentially Christian, bourgeois atmosphere, and the jolliness of the coloured drawings that accompanied the show was not intended to confront but to reassure. Moreover, the thoroughness of Asplund and his collaborators, well bedded in the tradition of building quickly but beautifully in wood, suggested the evocation of lightness and charm as an inevitable

Ernst May, H Boehm, E + O Fucker and F Thyriot, Siedlung Riederwald, Frankfurt, Germany, 1926–8. View from west: pencil on tracing paper, 29 x 93 cm. Deutsches Architekturmuseum Collection, Frankfurt/Maine.

Gunnar Asplund, Stockholm Exhibition, Sweden, 1930.

subplot. The Swedish penchant for extending the Modernist aesthetic through furniture and industrial design, and eventually retreating in their architecture towards nuance rather than statement, illustrates this.

The thin tower made up of lights is surely a pioneer work – serving as it did for the next 70 years as a model for urban situations in every developed country. The wispy architecture was picked up by those cultures relaxed enough to treat it seriously – the West Coast of the US or Australia, for instance. Yet in the drawing shown here there is also that sweet, almost coy Nordic Romanticism that can be found in the minimal decoration that adorned the edges of Swedish Neoclassical surfaces: a world that Asplund himself knew well. Sometimes we have to stare hard at such a drawing and take on board all the conscious and subconscious conversations that are absorbed into its apparent carefree mode.

The same observation can be made of German architect, painter and set designer Hans Poelzig's highly atmospheric interior drawing for the Salzburg Festival Hall (1920–22). We are transported into the world of a kind of wonderland. Poelzig was an architect of insatiable imagination who at last had the opportunity to make a major interior space for this Austrian city

(his credentials already demonstrated at an extraordinary formalistic level in buildings for Posnan and Breslau). He suggested a magical place, that somehow avoided frippery. Aware of the power as well as the potential nuance of light with the pencil, being more than adequate for the description of its atmosphere. Able to span the distance between formed edges and lit surfaces with a mixture of ambiguity and clarity (we shall see this again in the work of Mark West, later on). Maybe it is only pencil that can adequately both suggest and describe with a wilfulness that is not often captured by the computer. One almost expects a magical response from the audiences, too, that they exist as tricky, chattering inhabitants of a Beckmann or Kirchner painting – but in black and white, of course.

If Stockholm had to be charmed and Salzburg had to be stimulated, then how should a confident but somewhat materialistic Midwest of the 1930s be engaged by the new architecture? While Tennessee-born abstract artist Weimer Pursell's poster for the Chicago World's Fair of 1933 is in no way in the tradition of architects' visions, it nonetheless captures the essential rhetoric of the event for its own particular audience. The forms, and even the small, more visionary sub-pictures at the bottom of the poster, avoid

Hans Poelzig, Festspielhaus (Festival Hall), Salzburg, Austria, 1920–2.

Weimer Pursell, Chicago World's Fair, 1933. Deutsches Architekturmuseum Collection, Frankfurt/Main.

anything too surprising and could easily be parts of factories or office blocks going up in town. It is all presented in a jolly, bright, middlebrow scheme of orange, blue, pea-green and only a little bit of black. Rhetorical red is even avoided. It is the new architecture as a pleasant, acceptable idea – here in a city that had long since harboured the fearlessness of Louis Sullivan and Frank Lloyd Wright.

Extending the Cultural Limits

If I am implying that the exposure of atmosphere and expression is often the subconscious declaration of the background culture, I am also suggesting that the role of much of this work is to extend the pre-existent range of the architecture available. Thus it has a two-way obligation, and for every one person making the depiction (usually, but not always the named architect) with a consciousness of this role, there is another who unwittingly reveals the limitations of that culture.

Takehiko Nagakura, computer graphics visualisation of *Paradiso of the Danteum* (Giuseppe Terragni and Pietro Lingeri, 1938), MIT, Cambridge, Massachusetts, US, 1999.

Hugh Ferriss, Arts Centre (Metropolis of Tomorrow), c. 1928. Photomechanical reproduction on paper.

By the end of the 20th century, it became possible to manipulate the capture of images in such a way that the two-way obligation becomes a creative base in its own right. Contemplating Tokyo-born architect Takehiko Nagakura's 1999 computer graphics visualisation from a 1938 film entitled *Paradiso of the Danteum*, the possibilities with digital manipulation of as-found material are visible. The photograph of a real place can be re-created as a new form. Reality can be manipulated towards, effectively, a drawing. The concept of 'back-and-forth' between reality and detachment from reality is exciting here because it passes through a 'freezeable', recordable condition and does not have to rely on the memory of the human brain. It is in essence an artificial aid to the transformation process. The full implications of this phenomenon are yet to be realised.

Without such means, we return to the monochrome hand graphic developed in the 1930s and 1940s by Hugh Ferriss as a means of dramatising the massing and heroics of the American skyscraper to a state of both worldliness and otherworldliness (see also his Fisher Building in Chapter 3.) Surely the genre of the high building organised to take account of the light-zoning

Bruce Goff, Single-Family House, 1935. Interior perspective of dining room: pencil and coloured pencil on tracing paper, 16.5 x 31.5 cm.

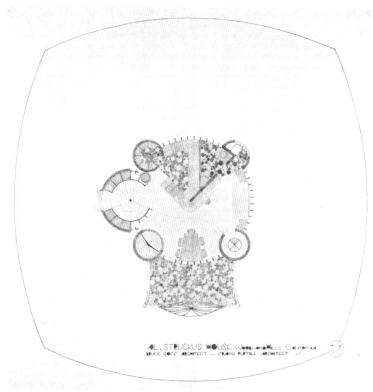

Bruce Goff and Frank Purtoll, Al Struckus House, Woodland Hills, California, US, 1979–81. First-floor plan: coloured and airbrushed photocopy, 45.9 x 45.8 cm. Deutsches Architekturmuseum Collection, Frankfurt/Main.

laws was already well known, yet Ferriss found a way of celebrating it in the same way as the sets for the film *Metropolis* had done in 1927 in Germany. By elegantly subsuming the detail, he increased the heroic quality of the whole. One's suspicion is that in many of his commissions to make perspectives of New York proposals, Ferriss was anyway not supplied with detailed information. His task was to tantalise and celebrate. The avoidance of minutiae served the strength of his charcoal atmospherics.

That he could nonetheless hold on to communicating the scale of the objects raises a quaint irony of expression and atmospherics in all this work. Several examples – Hadid, Alsop, Ferriss and others – choose to bypass the pedantry of detail and in so doing hold on to the thrust of the project. Yet scale is highly necessary in validating a drawing as architecture rather than general-purpose illustration. How to introduce clues of scale without a chatter of little bits and pieces is one of the hardest tasks of drawing – at least as far as 20th- and 21st-century taste is concerned. Much has been written elsewhere about the 'selective eye', and the issue certainly resonated within the territory of architecture.

Shifting Position

Over time, the same architects can change emphasis and position. I was intrigued, therefore, to come upon two drawings by an architect who was never a mere follower of fashion. Bruce Goff is generally treated as a Midwestern eccentric and inventor – off on a tangent from his mentor, Frank Lloyd Wright – but his span was greater than this description supplies. His drawing for a Single-Family House of 1935 contains no charm. Indeed, it is clumsily made, yet now possesses a period attraction. Once shown his book collection (which contained the whole set of the Wasmuth *Blauen Bücher* from 1920s Berlin), I recognise the influences at work in his early years. The interior is a form of stripped-down Modernism (with just the odd hint of Wright) and, like the Frankfurt housing by May and his friends, Goff feels the need to draw only in a simple way.

More than 40 years on, Goff created another drawing for a family: the Al Struckus House in Woodland Hills, California (1979–81). This time it is a plan and has much of the richness that we might expect from a painting by Gustav Klimt. The indulgence of the paving (or is it tiling?) pattern is no mere decoration. There is a relaxed enjoyment of circular geometry and, for the connoisseur, no mean handling of it. It is at first sight a decorative piece. At second sight it contains a strong character. There is no need to delve into the three-dimensional implications at this moment: let us enjoy the carefree ambience that can be expected of this house and its implicitly rich lifestyle. All done with a plan drawing.

Architectural Narrative

Through architectural drawings of a certain kind, stories can also be told.

Using quite conventional techniques, but brilliantly wrought, Luke Chandresinghe, (who won the RIBA President's Medal when he graduated from the Bartlett School of Architecture, UCL, London, in 2004 with his Institute of Ideas), composes two sidewalls and a kiln-like end piece to suggest a place in which dramatic issues are discussed or invoked in some way. The descent of fragments that reveal themselves to be newspapers adds to the suggestion of event. At first the drawing here has a single focus and atmosphere, but then there are a number of knowing additions that increase the intrigue of the place. First, the spring-like technical divide at the top of the 'kiln'. Then a realisation that the flanking walls are more complex than we at first thought, revealing gradually a series of strands that are not just running up and down but attaching themselves as discrete racking or spacing elements. Further observation notices an occasional diagonal strand and a holding element or two. If you look at the drawing long enough you begin to question almost every characteristic by which you first assessed it.

We have been led to believe the unbelievable through drawing. Now we are tempted to set up in our minds a series of belief/disbelief/belief/disbelief. We are itching to know the story for it is both an architectural space and a scenographic construct. The same is true of Samuel White's haunting interior Chapel to the Corpus (2004) that is produced by skilful coaxing of the computer.

That both these drawings were produced within the same architectural school only a year or so apart speaks of the mood of architectural pursuit, but also of a liberal culture in which neither one is considered more exploratory nor more graphic than the other. Their appropriateness is in the way in which the artist feels able to control his technique in such a way as to provide us with the tangible and the not-quite-so-tangible together. White's interior feels like a theatre fly-tower gone mad. A certain regularity of the carrying devices is jerked out of its comfortableness by the sinister nature of the

Luke Chandresinghe, The
Institute of Ideas, Lower Lea
Valley, east London, UK, 2006.
View from central corridor
of storage tower looking
towards the expiration vessel:
collage, acrylic and ink on paper,
21 x 21 cm.

hanging figures. There is a further layer of questions set up by the machines, and the racks add menace – though might, just, offer an explanation.

The choice of the yellow tone is appropriate: suggesting release, or at least the presence of the sun up there somewhere. The gradual dissolution of objects as they become fogged over by the light is another intriguing device enabling some of the parts to be seen – or rather surmised as ambiguous presences – once again presenting us with an imperceptible bridge between architecture and the dramatic moment.

Drawing, the technique of making drawings (by whatever means) and the expression of atmosphere have now reached such a state of interaction that we can once again dream what we wish and only have to follow through with built form. In the past we could only talk about it and let the observer dwell too much on the issue of appropriate devices to sustain the idea. As our resource of devices, seen and unseen, widens, so can we respond.

Drawing and Technics

The tradition of the architects' 'technical drawing' lies historically at a watershed. The smartest and fastest builders are increasingly passing their instructions directly from the predictive computer stage to the fabrication point. A set of parametric intentions can be linked directly to cutters, modellers, printers, evacuators or even patches of space that can have material induced into them. Perhaps it will be a long time before the designer stops making jottings, scribbles, rough layouts or cartoons of the procedure and the profile of things, but the conscious formalisation of drawn instructions is probably on the wane.

Against this lies that accumulated fascination of architects themselves – and not a few architectural supporters – with the physical inspiration of technology: that magic of bits and pieces, of things that do things. 'Action' was an inspiration for many great projects of the 20th century, leading to those gyrating solids and onwards to the notion of time as a tectonic element. The machine led to the device, to the gadget, and to a manner of thinking by which the hinge becomes far more expressive than the door.

We are now past the heyday of 'High-Tech' architecture, which has matured into a form of international vernacular for the upmarket corporate building. More often we seem to be demanding of technically loaded buildings that they remain discrete about it. In a world where the actual point of control is in a tiny chip in a hidden circuit, there is something sweet but quaint about our continued desire to celebrate the working part or the constructed technique. Yet within this paradox lies a delightful stream of architectural investigation, architectural expression and, of course, architectural invention.

We are reminded often enough that the Doric, Ionic and Corinthian orders were derived from the fundamental elements of our trees and forests and have hung around as a symbolic language for rather a long time. So why not celebrate the hinge, the hook and the gusset? Alongside these is that edgy territory that engages or disengages the relationship of the architect and the engineer. Classic icons of our experience from the Eiffel Tower through the Centre Pompidou to the Beijing stadium not only question the creative autonomy of the architect, but throw open the issue of initiative. Without a generation or two of brilliant designer-engineers, the High-Tech movement could have never happened and the marvellous joints would exist in a creative vacuum.

Operational Drawings

Having contemplated Neil Denari's 1989 project for the Tokyo International Forum in Chapter 5 and discovered his clarity and boldness on a large scale, it is fascinating to watch him investigate a small-scale working part and consider how much his own design personality is able to jump down in scale and yet still be identifiable.

The Floating Illuminator (1992) is a light-projection device with a modicum of robotics. The two drawings – section/elevation and plan – are intricately drawn and annotated, but also have toned areas for identification. On closer inspection there are shadows and a shaded zone (the reflector), thus exposing this version as both an 'information' drawing and an 'art' drawing.

This last, rather loose epithet is often used in architectural circles to describe a drawing that may be used by the author for exhibitions and books, but where the 'useful' version has already become part of the working process.

However, for Denari, as with some other brilliant designers, it is difficult (and probably unnecessary) to disengage the information from the art. The appearance and the impact of the thing is inextricably folded into the inventive and technical aspects. At once we have hit another territory by which the state of architecture itself is exposed by an analysis of drawings.

Neil Denari, Floating Illuminator, 1992. Ink/airbrush on Mylar, 76.2 x 101.6 cm.

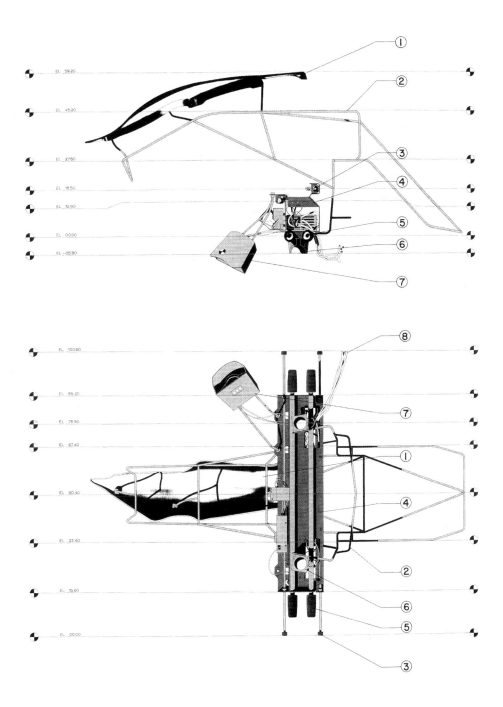

EL 59.20
EL 45.20
EL 27.60
EL 16.50
EL 12.60
EL 00.00
EL -05.60

①
②
③
④
⑤
⑥
⑦

EL 100.80
EL 85.20
EL 75.50
EL 67.40
EL 50.40
EL 33.40
EL 15.60
EL 00.00

⑧
⑦
①
④
②
⑥
⑤
③

More commercial or 'middlebrow' architects than most who appear in this book will produce design drawings and then pass the 'illustration' of the whole, or selected parts of the building, on to an in-house or out-of-house 'renderer'. In extreme cases this can now be someone on a computer in another continent. Given enough information to 'make it look interesting' (or whatever), if liked by the client, this disengaged illustrator may well have had more to do with the appearance of the built work than the rest of the team.

For Denari, this can never be so. Even this little gadget is of the project. It needs its shadows and shading and even, perhaps, its almost Victorian enjoyment of the personality of the ratchets and wires.

Enric Miralles and Benedetta Tagliabue (Miralles Tagliabue EMBT) and Inbo Adviseurs Bouw Amersfoort, Utrecht Town Hall, the Netherlands, 2000. Ground floor and second floor plans.

The late Catalan architect Enric Miralles, who is now often best known as the designer of the Scottish Parliament, had the ability to think and design in three dimensions to a rare degree; able to scribble a twisted roof or a strutting leg before it had had a chance to land onto the ground. What extraordinary creativity there was encompassed by mere operational drawings (I hesitate to merely call them 'working drawings'). In his designs for the renovations to Utrecht Town Hall (1997–2000), a whole lexicon of architecture is embodied in this straightforward technique of single lines indicating the position of objects, accompanied by straight lines indicating the dimensions of these objects. Yet there is an intense series of objectives at work: the layering, the tweaking – almost the caressing of the space by the range of Miralles' inventiveness.

The equally simply drawn version that shows some roofing and other upper-level structure reveals the project as a close-grained essay in control. The intricacy suddenly makes sense. The deadpan way in which trusses, studwork or steps are depicted lends a forensic quality to the whole project, thereby bridging the world of virtuosity in profile with that of the straightforwardness of craft. Yet if the drawings had been in any way self-conscious, the whole construct would appear indigestible. For the professional architect, such drawings can bring the same measure of delight and admiration as can the reading of a complex score by a musician.

If the tragedy of Miralles was his early demise (but a legacy of several brilliant structures), that of Russian Constructivist Ivan Léonidov was to survive as a menial workshop instructor in the Moscow Academy of Architecture decades after the publication in 1934 of the famous Narkomtiazhprom project, his competition design for the Commissariat of Heavy Industry for Red Square in Moscow. Several versions exist, but the drawing shown here is intriguing for its relative pedantry of detail. It reveals a remarkable level of know-how on Léonidov's part: the trusses are carefully scaled and placed, the bracing is discrete but adequate, and the system of triangulated props anticipates mannerisms that would become fashionable 40 years later.

As with the Denari drawings, there is a subtle combination of straightforward information and 'modelling' – the indication of shade and shadow. Here, it is introduced gradually upwards on the drawing, so that the tops reveal the form and one's brain is quite capable of extrapolating this information downwards. More than anything, it reveals to us the seriousness with which Léonidov took his architecture, known for his concepts that

Ivan Léonidov, Commissariat of Heavy Industry (Narkomtiazhprom), Moscow, Russia, 1934. Perspective looking north along the Red Square elevation towards the Bolshoi Theatre: ink and watercolour on paper, 182.2 x 117.5 cm.

involved pyramids, airships and (as we can see) a certain audacity with which he treats a brief for a Commissariat building. Here the components are essential to the discourse.

Architecture as Body-Wrap

Even more essential were the working parts of Michael Webb's Suitaloon (1967), which must, in a way, include the depicted humans as such. The chassis elements and the tube-skin elements are tracked as a series of metamorphoses take place. The project takes gadgetry to the status of high art – but even further to the status of generator of the entire project. The

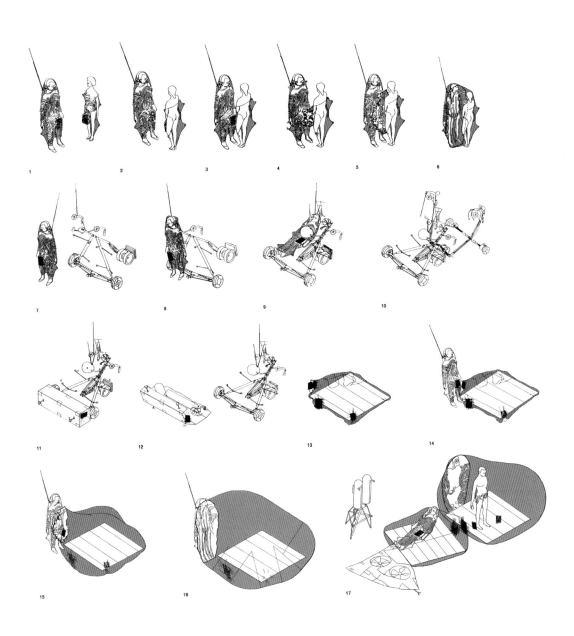

1   2   3   4   5   6

7   8   9   10

11   12   13   14

15   16   17

Michael Webb, Suitaloon, 1967.
Ink line and coloured overlay on
paper, 59 x 50 cm.

straightforward nature of the drawings themselves recalls the diagrams in an instruction booklet for an appliance or an Ikea procedure. Webb is rather keen on this approach and it serves to point out both the internal logic of the thing and the power of the idea, without the need for surface attractiveness or any other rendering.

The project is immensely challenging, for it allies the technology and the existence of the concept of 'structure' to a psychological moment. The dream of two people. By its very name, also, we must remember that the other point of origin is the suit itself. Garment to building … garment through dream to building, even.

Julia Von Rohr, Colour Interface, 1999.

Almost 35 years later, as an adjunct to the larger Natural Dyefactory and Aromatherapy Bath-house project that won her a Student Silver Medal for Drawing in the RIBA President's Medals of 1999, Julia Von Rohr, in her Colour Interface (also 1999) continues the theme of architecture as an environmental body-wrap. An array of illuminated points that are reminiscent of a synthesiser relate together with a keypad and a sound system. Such a project is now able to be digitally rendered so that we can easily believe that the wearable reflective scarf and sociable heating balloon devices could be available in our favourite warehouse. Again, the artist is extremely deft in her intensification and then de-intensification of the image, holding the human just there, and just perceptibly female.

Tectonic and Representational Range

We now have so many presentational techniques available to us that any particular choice of method can be scrutinised and discussed by the cognoscenti – almost as an issue of partisanship. Architects are, and always have been, conscious of the parallel state of fine art: hence the uneasy quote of the 'art drawing'. It can also be argued that Modernism (in the hands of the Russian Constructivists, the Dutch of the 1920s and 1930s and Le Corbusier himself – who was, after all, a half-day painter) owes so much to art movements. Perhaps more pernicious – or less theoretical – is the sideways influence of graphic design and publicity graphics. After all, architects wish to be understood and are the children of their local culture and their generation. Ex-Archigram member Michael Webb, when still new to the US in 1965, made a project, Rent-a-Wall, that was a direct commentary on American sales techniques. He has also, over a long career, developed a series of techniques: pencil, ink, neo-advertising, oil painting, collage and the rest as a part of his constant exploration.

The same is true of CJ Lim, who explores design, extending his tectonic range alongside the development of his presentational range. In the World of Cow project (2000) he combines very simple line drawings together in such a way to emphasise key moments in a procedure. His 'eye' is impeccable, so the result never falls short of the 'elegant', but the creativity and audacity of the project – as we saw also with Webb's Suitaloon – is heightened by the straightforwardness of the drawing. There is no need for tonal or surface decoys. The solidity of the ground and the main parts appearing in section are heightened by reversing the lines as white upon red. This calls to mind the much-lamented charm of the old 1950s 'blueprint' where the white line against the blue background became popularly synonymous with the notion of 'technicality', and the term 'blueprint' is still used with this in mind.

On the right-hand side of the drawing a key moment in the process of delivering the cow is captured by black and grey lines, with the cow remaining white. The final three-dimensional view also uses that palette. Imperceptibly, a three-colour range has crept into an apparently one-colour situation. Lim is the child of a world in which more people will see the work in a book than will ever see the original drawing: so minimum inking and overlay printing breeds a conscious (and eventually subconscious) use of this for both clarification and economy. Such demands have always affected architectural drawing. The etchings of Piranesi, the silkscreens of Chernikov, and the digitalised folds of 21st-century Hadid respond to the reproductive technology that feeds back to the aesthetics of the notions themselves. It is an inevitable loop.

In his The Hanging Gardens of Wanton Harmony (2000), Lim extends the range to take on the necessary coloration to deal with the plantation itself.

CJ Lim/Studio 8, World of Cow, London, UK, 2000. Sketches: pen and ink on film.

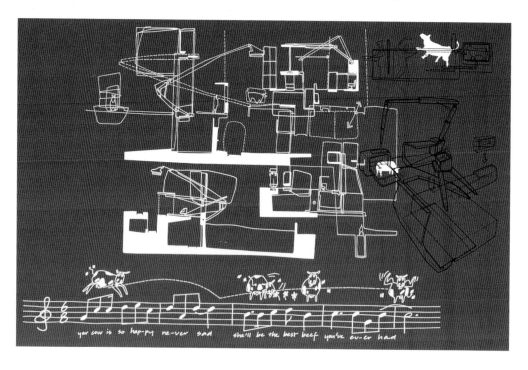

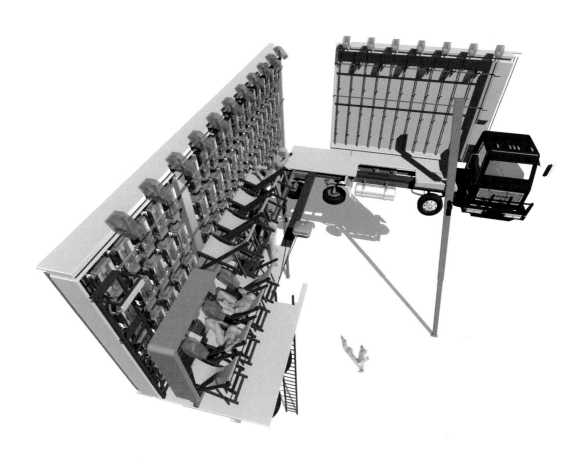

CJ Lim/Studio 8, The Hanging Gardens of Wanton Harmony, London Suburbia, UK, 2000. Top view of modified HGV with a wall of hemp plants: computer render.

Vegetation, as with water, loses much of its challenge and role play vis-à-vis 'hardware' in an architectural project unless it can be seen in colour.

The 1990s were in many ways a turning point in the discussion of drawing. The computer was beginning to establish a leading position, the discussion of 'process' was rampant in the most fashionable schools of architecture, the gadget was a creative trigger, the absorption of photographics, multitudinous printing techniques and the inspiration of film and video led to spirited discussion of architecture and its presence or non-presence. Contemplating (say) a rectangular surface in front of you did not necessarily mean that you would be offered a total, retainable or definite image.

That such an image might 'melt' or metamorphose was the basis of the installation *The Desiring Eye* by the New York designers Elizabeth Diller and Ricardo Scofidio at Gallery MA in Tokyo in 1992, and later at the Venice Biennale. The apparatus enabled the imagery to fog over and fade and then reappear progressively. The creation later by Diller Scofidio + Renfro of the Blur Building on Lake Neuchâtel for the 2002 Swiss Expo, in which a built structure disappears from view within a large cloud of water spray,

Diller + Scofidio, The Desiring Eye, Gallery MA, Tokyo, 1992.

Nat Chard, Variable Picture Plane drawing instrument 02, 2006. Cast aluminium, glass, acrylic and MDF.

continued the proposition out of drawn form and into reality. The assemblage thus becomes a technical drawing manifest as a technicality manifest as a participatory event – as an environment in itself.

Work continues in the territory of physical investigation of perception and the process of making a drawing in the work of Canada-based British architect and professor Nat Chard who, in addition to setting up experiments with various groups of students where optical devices (cameras in which you draw onto the photograph as you take the picture) and perception machines have been developed, has worked on drawing machines of various kinds. The transfer of initiative and response back and forth between viewer, significant moment, image and tracking or 'capturing' device is now under scrutiny, giving drawing itself a niche within the investigatory world of technology.

Subtle Technology and Nuance

There are simple renderings that look plausible and seductive, enabling us to accept the achievement of quite radical technology as an unremarkable

phenomenon. So we look at young London-based, Hong Kong architect Billy Choi's Immersion drawing for the Blizzard in Hong Kong project (2006) as a reasonable idea, and we know that the waving strands can be achieved using recently developed materials. In no way is the drawing a shrill call for the new technology. Perhaps at this point we have reached a stage in the game whereby technics can return to being a given: a natural part of architecture as it must be enjoyed.

Billy Choi, Immersion, Blizzard in Hong Kong – A Material Intervention of Visual and Spatial Experience in the City, Kowloon, Hong Kong, 2006. Computer-generated and synthesised digital image.

Such nonchalance is always more likely within an urban setting: the artificial 'blizzard' is proposed for a part of Hong Kong that is already full of contemporary wonders and a fulsome absorption of technology. The old adrenaline buzz returns with more force once we stray away from the city, and even more so if we start to combine contexts and traditions. The gadget or device to reinforce husbandry is now well established in the irrigation of near-deserts or of sluggish gardens. Extending this to a visible forest of robotics with a far more ambitious programme of transformation celebrates both the potential of valves, timers, air, water and fertilisers as a hybrid force, but renders the key element itself back into the heroic role of the tree or the spring as generator.

Making the appropriate drawing, albeit with the computer as the available device, demands a certain subtlety. Yukihiko Sugawara, a young Japanese architect who graduated from the Bartlett School of Architecture, UCL, London, in 2004, chooses carefully: in 'misting' the landscape, rendering it somewhat ambiguous, endless, and mysterious, he seduces us into a certain benign comprehension of it all. This was far less possible for earlier generations of techno-addicts. We were all so excited by the formal possibilities of the gadget that we tended to over-draw them, caring little for immersion unless it was total or playing with the idea of decoy – as in Log Plug or Rock Plug (1968) by fellow Archigramer David Greene. What we now have is a reciprocal role played by the various parts whether vegetal, technical or hybrid. Looking again at the drawing we begin to suspect some of the stones or pebbles of being robotic – but without apprehension.

All the time, however, there are the mannerisms of the devices and the period out of which they have come. It is not a question of styling: that would be too crude. It is not only a question of technique: although we shall continue to bounce the subject of technique in and out of the narrative. It may somehow be a question of nuance. An assumption of how much the observer wishes to be told, how much he or she already knows, how much else needs to be alluded to. Creative laziness comes into it as well. Why should a designer bother to draw or explain more of the idea than is strictly necessary? Perhaps it is useful to keep the observer guessing. Perhaps it can be a more selfish instinct whereby the person drawing is doing it for his or her investigatory purposes and – if they are interested – passers-by can make of it what they will.

Yukihiko Sugawara, Bio-topia Induced by Terra-diversification System, 2004. Pencil, airbrush and photography in Photoshop.

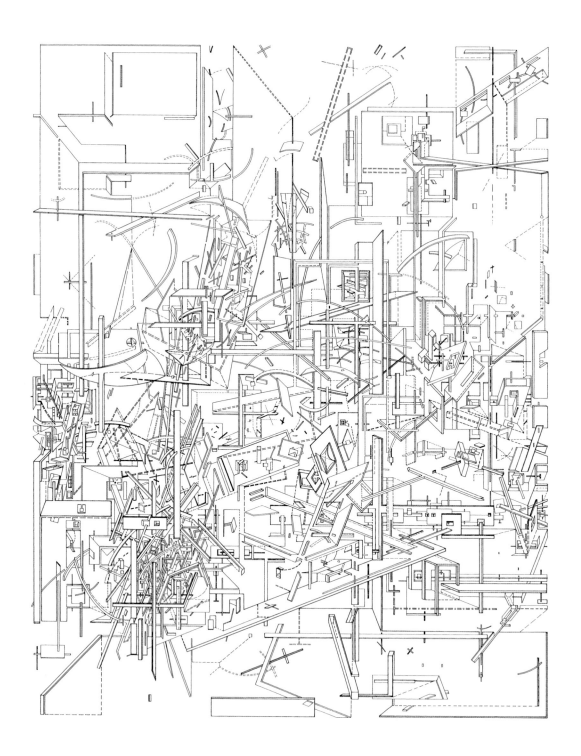

Daniel Libeskind, Little Universe,
1979. Ink on paper.

The career of Daniel Libeskind has been riddled with extraordinary manifestations, from drawings, installations, buildings through statements and musical performance. In choosing to illustrate Little Universe (1979), a modest and intriguing piece of armature, one can make the point that inventive energy and the drawing can be uncannily compounded – if the talent is there.

The Plant (1995), a pencil drawing by Canadian architect and academic Mark West is, however, far more sinister. It is a love affair with the technical – the wall on the right is both techno-inventive and military in overtone – and

Mark West, The Plant, 1995.
Graphite on paper, 29 x 37 cm.

simultaneously a critique of industrialisation and production. The mannerism is curious in being neither radical, nor commonplace, nor retrospective. It is self-contained: neither animate nor latent. One can surmise that the soldier-like vessels are inflatables and are the particular interest of the artist. The left-hand side of the drawing seems to be deliberately taken from the world of satanic mills. Out of such work has come West's significant contribution to the world of concrete surfaces and how they can be manipulated, so we must consider this drawing as both an intellectual reflection and a preliminary sortie into a world of formulation.

Drawing in Process

The role of drawings in the making of a slightly unorthodox building is in itself an endless and ruleless discussion. The conception of the Kunsthaus Graz in Austria (2000) was relatively traditional. Colin Fournier and myself sat with our colleagues for several weeks at the competition stage in early 2000 and, once the basic idea had been established, acted as editors for the daily cycle of computer-logged plans and sections. After winning the competition, moving into production mode did not at first change the procedure, but gradually optimal conditions began to occur, making demands on the business of drawing and tracking/tracking and drawing: landing the nozzles on to a surface that was distorting in several directions at once, wrapping the skin around in an elegant way, incorporating the pixelated light system. Wrapping and cutting, cutting and wrapping. A system of three-dimensional computer drawing was evolved to log the state of play so that it could constantly be reviewed.

The resultant drawings are therefore both creative and reflective, but essentially ongoing. Without rhetoric but certainly authentic. They held a special role for the integration of work, made in Frankfurt by structural engineers Bollinger + Grohmann, Colin and myself in London and the production office in Graz. Such 'presentation' drawings as there were became superfluous and were nearly always inferior to the object that was rapidly emerging from the ground. Despite this, the building bears a strong resemblance to that made as pencil sketches at the outset. The three-dimensional, coloured, linear drawings remain as a link to the memory of the process.

In this way one experiences drawing as a commentary. Perhaps it was always so: and in particular with technical inspiration.

Peter Cook and Colin Fournier, Kunsthaus Graz, Austria, 2000. First-floor plan (main gallery), competition stage version: computer-generated drawing.

Peter Cook and Colin Fournier: architects; Klaus Bollinger and Manfred Grohmann: structural engineers. Kunsthaus Graz, Austria, 2000. Cutaway diagram showing structure and main componenting.

Peter Cook and Colin Fournier, Kunsthaus Graz, Austria, 2000. Detail of three-dimensional form around roof nozzles: computer-generated drawing.

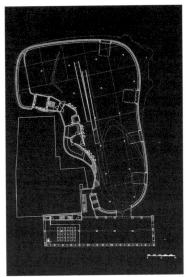

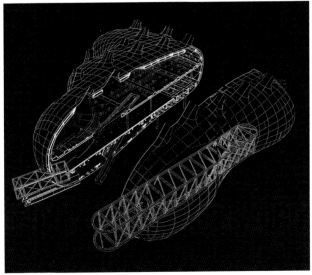

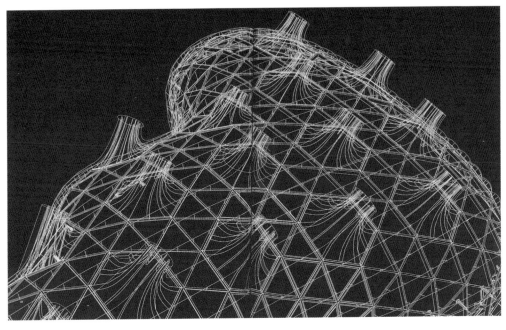

8
Drawing and Surface

The Tyrolean artist Walter Pichler exercises a pivotal role in the history of architectural drawing of the late 20th century. Exponents of the art as different as Peter Wilson, Michael Webb or Lebbeus Woods refer not only to the haunting quality of his subject matter, but more to the range of expression that the substance of the drawing itself can expose. On occasion Pichler has been known to deliberately screw up the densest of paper (produced in Germany as 'Schoelles *Hammer Papier*'), draw rapidly across the imperfect surface and then add colour, progressively combining the continuity of the main theme of the drawing and the existence of the damage – or rather the 'wounding' of – the drawing.

Pichler has lived for many years in both Vienna and at St Martin in Burgenland, in rural eastern Austria, where in the yard of his farm he has constructed a series of small buildings tailored around his sculpted works and possessing intensely calculated conditions of light and space. Intriguingly he has paid for these buildings in part from the income of the sale of the drawings made to propose and explain those same buildings.

This is surely a rare occurrence. His earlier work ran somewhat parallel to that of his friend, the architect Hans Hollein. Both were preoccupied with the idea of cities that could be set into the ground, with the invention of environmental helmets and with the predicament of 'the body'. Pichler, who also has had success as a designer of artefacts and books, was nonetheless to take the brooding speculation whereby the soil, the artefact, the bones of the body and the threatened flesh become immersed in a series of necrogenic speculations. The Vienna Actionists, Günter Brus and Hermann Nitsche, are the extreme exponents of these speculations – prepared to create around the bodies of animals and even to attack their own bodies. By comparison, Pichler's sculpted pieces where fractured bones of animals are augmented by deliciously fashioned metal additions are more gentle. The drawings move inwards and outwards of the most intense combinations: and move further outwards towards the more dry depiction of wooden or brick structures. Yet the essence of the violent attack on the paper can be seen as a direct link. Moreover, there is the quality of the line itself: many times I have noticed a very particular 'Austrian' mode of racing the pencil (or pen) across the paper with an increased pressure at the end of the line – a form of attack that characterises the drawn work of Hans Hollein, Raimund Abraham, Volker Giencke and Günther Domenig.

It is Domenig who most readily pays homage to his friend Pichler, as does the Viennese film-maker Peter Kubelka who has explored the Austrian culture of 'body', 'decay', symbolic interference and attack in some of his cooking demonstrations.

Walter Pichler,
Augenschmerzen, St Martin,
Germany, 1979. Pencil and ink,
29.7 x 21.0 cm.

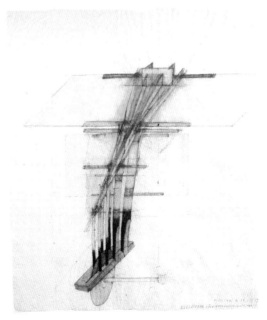

Walter Pichler's other interest has been in the lost cities of South America, which gave inspiration to much of his early work. So if we combine all these territories – forgotten, latent, threatened, constructed, fitted tightly, direct and symbolic – we observe a tremendous repository of reference to be matched by his peerless technique. Seen only in books and galleries (he refuses to lecture), Pichler nonetheless becomes a point of reference in any discussion of the power of the drawing.

His choice of colour revolves around a preference for browns and an almost implicit combination of 'rust' and 'tree bark' – if such a thing could exist. Grey and yellow are invoked as well, for particular occasions when 'precision' or 'brightness' emerge as desirable articulations. Most of his architect-followers, while intrigued by his intensity, choose to widen the palette and simultaneously find it difficult to hold on to his intensity.

One English admirer of Pichler's work is Christine Hawley who has herself from time to time tackled this same issue of the substance of the drawing. Possessing a natural ability to draw in the conventional sense (see her drawings for Shadow House in Chapter 4), she nonetheless became intrigued by the idea of not only combining a series of techniques within one flat surface, but of testing out just how near to the reality of the subject these techniques could go. Thus metal is represented by metal itself. Painted surface is represented by paint itself and, most interestingly, burned wood is represented by burned wood itself.

Arguably what we then have in her image of the Peckham House (1982) is a flattened model: yet unlike a model, there is no attempt to present three-dimensional parts. Even the tradition of bas-relief suggests that the parts are in a spatial relation to each other – it is just that these spaces are compressed – but are still there to be acknowledged.

So Hawley presents a 'sandwich' that combines tried-and-tested components with those less common – the line drawing, the silkscreen print – and, through the use of acetate sheet that is sometimes painted on the back, there can be areas of colour that are extremely intense since the effect of the acetate is to hold the colour tightly and give it additional gloss. The project to which this is applied concerns a proposal for a house in the run-down London district of Peckham where there were (at the time of the drawing in 1982), several burned-out houses.

Christine Hawley, Peckham
House, London, UK, 1982. TTS
print, hammerite paint, sand,
wire, acetate and acrylic paint,
150 x 100 cm.

Digital Dispassion

At this point it becomes tempting to contrast these very personal and material works with the relative dispassionateness of computer-generated surface. One can follow the manoeuvres of the group theverymany – made up of former students of the Architectural Association in London, notably Marc Fornes – a school that has recently focused on computer-generated systems and forms. Their work is not only among the most expressive of the genre, but in the series of studies illustrated gives a good clue as to the procedure that leads towards their range of flowerings. Subsequently they manipulate and divert the forms towards a series of tower propositions.

It is interesting to compare their towers with that of Sulan Kolatan and William MacDonald in Chapter 5: theverymany towers are more consistent and concerned, perhaps, to demonstrate the possibilities of a consistent set of manoeuvres. It could be that Kol/Mac, being of a slightly older generation of designers, see their dexterity of computer-generation as being a servant of the desire to make spaces, whereas the team theverymany are carried along by the 'magic' of the generative process itself.

In describing such work as 'dispassionate' I call attention to the combination of repeat and the monochromic. As with the buildings of Santiago Calatrava, the surface seems to need to be made of a single, endless, white material. Furthermore, the surface implies the kind of consistency that one sees

THEVERYMANY
www.theverymany.net

A(**n**)Y_001
Marc Fornes & Vincent Nowak & Claudia Corcilius

```
Option Explicit

Sub Timer()

' declare variables
Dim i, j
Dim arrPtsModel ' Dynamic array

' set variables: "fi" = Floor
Dim intFloorNumber : arrFloorNumber : 34
Dim arrFloorHeight : arrFloorHeight : r("random",1,1)(random(1,2))'4
Dim arrFloorRadius : arrFloorRadius : i(r(1)(1)("random",1,1.5))(1,1)'4

Dim varTopCollumn: intRadius(np + i(intFloorNumber) 0.6
Dim intpanel : ((4341 * )
```

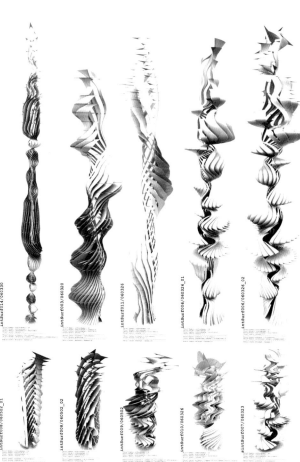

intSurf014/060330

intSurf013/060320

intSurf011/060326

intSurf006/060326_01

intSurf006/060326_02

intSurf008/060502_01

intSurf008/060502_02

intSurf009/060502

intSurf010/060326

intSurf007/060323

intSurf004/060323_02

intSurf004/060321_01

intSurf001/060320

intSurf002/060320

intSurf013/060328

intSurfTEST (tower9)

intSurfTEST (tower9)

intSurfTEST (tower9)

intSurfTEST (tower9)

intSurfTEST (tower9)

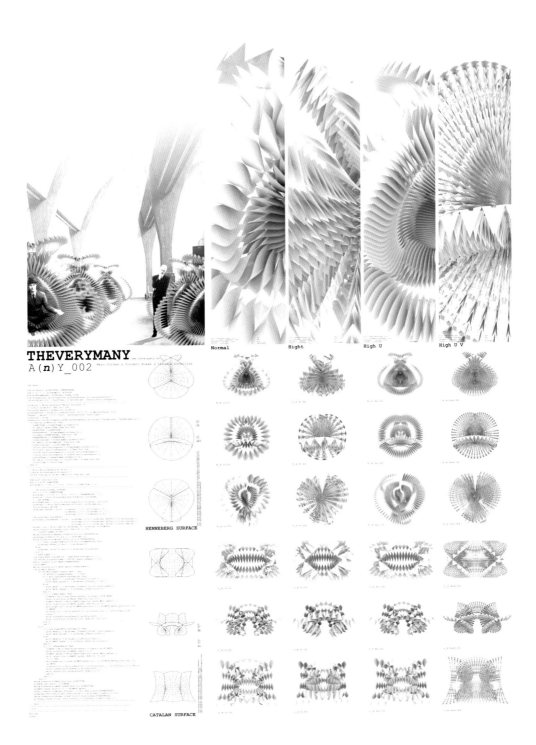

THEVERYMANY

A (*n*) Y_002

HENNEBERG SURFACE

CATALAN SURFACE

Normal

Hight

High U

High U V

in porcelain, ice or paper. Yet the feel of materiality is never far away: theverymany's Intsurf diagrams have a febrile quality, involving a range of thicknesses, intensities and hollowings-out. After all, these are analogous qualities to those that architects have always been seeking: the condition of intricacy and of particularity.

Since such work is created as mass rather than line, it is reasonable to suggest that there is less dependence on imitation or suggestion in the drawings produced. A single linkage of apparatus to the same generation of forms can produce cut or amassed solid objects. It could be that those solids are exactly as shown and exactly as consistent. If much is gained, is something lost?

This raises again the issue of drawing as ambition, plus the issue that many drawings suggest combinations of material and form that the architect hopes for, or wishes to happen. The cynics will comment that the result rarely comes up to scratch. The designer or visionary will argue that such drawings are part of the process of discovery (and certainly cheaper than building prototypes). Thus theverymany work unexpectedly shares, with the grubby, hand-coloured explorations, the essence of exploration.

Substance and Atmosphere

It is a late-modern view that the purpose of examining the quality of surface is not just to do with building, but is as much to do with the statement of atmosphere and nuance as are those grander drawings of whole edifices.

At this point we must look again at Lebbeus Woods – that most expressive of investigators, working both fluently but with considerable intellectual grit. Based for many years in New York, he had in the past worked on Roche-Dinkeloo's Ford Foundation building, and as a late 20th-century successor to Hugh Ferriss had made many perspectives for well-known New York offices. We have seen in Chapter 6 his ability to communicate both the substance and atmosphere of a building as well as its texture and materiality made him popular with the firms that used him who then maybe came to fear that the Woods rendition might prove to be superior in its quality and sensitivity to the building that actually happened.

Yet his true worth lies in his propositions: sometimes for cities that lived up in the sky, sometimes for more conveniently grounded structures. Sometimes

Marc Fornes with Vincent Novak and Claudia Corcilius, theverymany, exploration on explicit and encoded processes of growth, 2006.

apocryphal and usually propositional, his work can combine fine invention with the patina of the 'found' object – even the 'antique'.

From the time of his first independent exposure in Steven Holl's *Pamphlet Architecture* series in the 1990s, Woods' work became increasingly published and discussed by an ever-wider circle of students and young architects. His ability to describe ways in which to draw simply and quickly led to his work as a teacher and critic: all the time, meanwhile, expanding his vocabulary of form and power of attack. Sometimes quoted as comparing his visionary work to that of the cinema, his moments of 'frame' and 'burst' seem to draw even more from those incidents than you get on his drawn surfaces: the near-blemish, the near-crack or the strange little projecting nugget. By 2006 he has arrived at a new power and astringency with conflict space #1 (2006). The intensity of 'position' has taken over from 'patina'.

By now, we can regard Michael Webb as a consummate explorer – of territories, of concepts, of mechanics, of totally original combinations and, not least, of drawing techniques that he often devises specifically for the matter in hand. In a discussion of architectural substance and the way in which drawing can identify it, his early work had already established a fine definition. That it has continued to be at the cutting edge of investigation

Lebbeus Woods, Conflict Space #1, 2006. Crayon on linen.

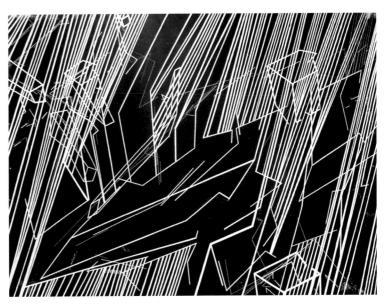

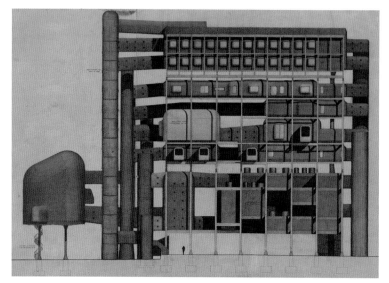

Michael Webb, Furniture
Manufacturers Association
Headquarters, High Wycombe,
UK, 1957–8. Side elevation:
graphite and ink on tracing
paper, mounted on board,
59.7 x 81.3 cm.

has never dulled his wish to push the potential of the medium – sometimes
pencil, sometimes oil paint, occasionally maquette, often a combination of
materials and techniques that occasionally include collage.

At this point, however, I would like to refer to his student project of 1958
that was a fourth-year task at the (then) Regent Street Polytechnic. Involving
a mannerism which, along with that of some other classmates, came to be
referred to by Reyner Banham as 'Bowellism', the Furniture Manufacturers
Association Headquarters (1957–8) is a giant rack through which are
threaded the chambers of varying categories.

An accompanying technical report concentrates on the use of 'Ferro cemento'
in which the cement is sprayed onto a mesh. The desire is for a universal and
rather plastic condition rather than the particularisation that is generated
by the precasting or in-situ casting of concrete – which inevitably reveals
joints. Of course, the lift shafts are shuttered concrete and the drawing
enjoys the revelation of this, just as it does with the variations of method by
which this nonetheless monochrome building would be made. The other
key achievement is that of pedantically defining the 'roundness' and three-
dimensionality of the parts. The shadows are boldly cast, in this respect
making interesting comparison with the elevations of Neil Denari (see
Chapters 5 and 7), similarly a fearless user of shadow projection.

Elaboration and Overstatement

In some ways the Victorian architect Arthur Beresford Pite in his Design for a West End Club House (1882) is as determined as Webb to define exactly the manner of the surface of his building: though to different ends. The overriding intention seems to have been one of creating a Romantic and picturesque world (look at the surrounding buildings: can the West End of London really have been as deliciously kooky as that in the late 19th century?). Such a mannerism creeps all over the surface of the building and Pite knowingly and fanatically knots and weaves, scratches and flaps this and that onto (and sometimes into) the general composition, creating a Gothic castle that demands the use of the pen or the etching plate to play out this scratching action.

It raises the question of medium and creative act – as well as medium and representational act. Pichler mutates: sometimes within the paper. Hawley captures the materials and theverymany push the process. Woods establishes the conventions and then breaks them. Webb seeks to define and Pite feverishly indulges.

Such indulgence allows the whole surface of the drawing to reach out to the observer, never letting one rest for a second, and somewhat in the manner of an illustrative cartoon feeds in many intriguing and diverting minutiae. We can ponder upon the various conditions of the stonework or features of someone's backyard.

Again, total in its creation of atmosphere and condition, while still in monochrome, whereas I myself could not have imagined making the project for the Medina Circle Tower in Tel Aviv (1997) without the extensive use of colour. It is not that the sky in Tel Aviv is red; rather that the warmth of the climate and the wish to articulate the profile ran together with a semi-conscious statement about the volatility and entrepreneurship of the locals. Moreover, the red colour establishes a palette that can incorporate shades of blue, purple and a kind of pink that serve to illustrate key constituents: windows, screens, sun blinds and shadowy interior forms.

The basic proposition is of three towers to occupy the upmarket location of the Medina Circle in North Tel Aviv. It was originally designed with the cooperation of Oscar Niemeyer, whose intention was always that the big

ROYAL INSTITVTE OF
BRITISH ARCHITECTS
SOANE 1893
Medallion
PRIZE Design

A WEST-END
CLVB-HOVSE

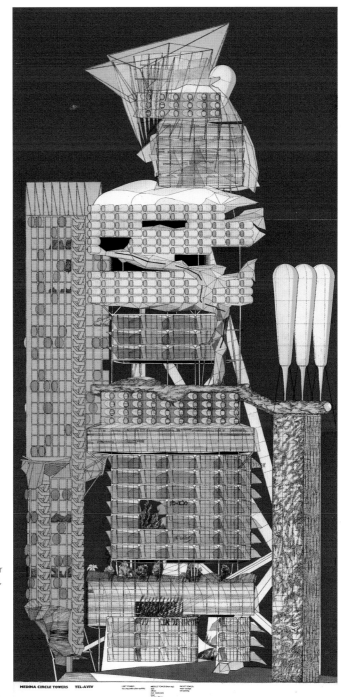

MEDINA CIRCLE TOWERS   TEL-AVIV

ELEVATION 1:200

Arthur Beresford Pite, Design for
a West End Club House, London,
UK, 1882. Exterior, black and
white drawing. RIBA Library
Drawings Collection.

Peter Cook, Medina Circle
Tower, Tel Aviv, Israel, 1997.
Elevation: line drawing with
watercolour and small areas of
coloured pencil, background in
pantone, 140 x 35 cm. Collection
of the Royal Academy of Arts,
London.

circle of shops and apartments should contain some towers within it. So far this has not happened. My composition is of a housing tower (discretely in the rear, in pink), the vegetated racking of a parking tower and a primary tower made up of 10 different categories of entrepreneurial activity: offices, showrooms, hotels, consultancies etc. Each type with differing requirements and differing facade characteristics. Each articulated from the other and threaded together like a vertical kebab.

There are some local incidents, deviations and appendages – though far fewer than would satisfy Beresford Pite. There is an emphasis on the glassy quality of much of the building, and the basic line drawing is mostly coloured in watercolour, which I always find to be both highly controllable and capable of reconsideration as one proceeds. It enables one to gauge the degree of contrast or the degree of 'filming' over the preceding layer of colour.

Such a drawing is therefore quite conventionalised, as befits a propositional work. It is in some ways slightly overstating the situation, drawing attention to the relation between programme and form.

Peter Cook and Christine Hawley, Museum of Stained Glass, Langen, Germany, 1986. Pencil, ink and watercolour. 60 x 40 cm.

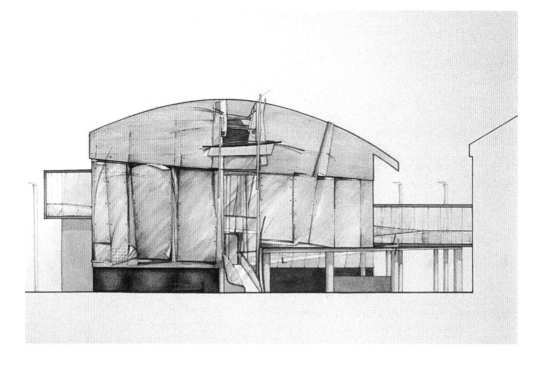

Conveying Character

In an earlier work made together with Christine Hawley, the programme was more homogeneous, but the desire on the elevation drawing was to discuss the quality of material and surface. The Museum of Stained Glass for Langen in Germany (1986) is a form of 'art shed' – deliberately modest, though with a sophisticated set of juxtapositions of space around a winding series of ramps. The role of this particular elevation (drawn by Christine) is to reassure the quiet old street that the new building is far from being brash or combative. The main body sits above the discrete base, which houses a youth room and a wine cellar. The narrow cut invites you in to progressively climb and discover the glass exhibits. Only one glass construction sits as a marker over the entrance gap. It is a sheet-steel building with some folding and rippling of the steel encouraged. The pencil-work and modest use of bright colour is there to both reassure and intrigue. The desire to manipulate the metal is developed through the drawing, as are the occasional splays and twigs intended to be steel articulations.

In some ways this drawn exploration is talking very much about mannerism and character, the form having been established before. The discussion of it as a 'shed', with memories of the outbuildings at Bennington College in Vermont, or as a 'quiet' building – though with an athletic looking circulation – needed to be explored. Such a drawing is supposed to be for public presentation, but is used by the authors to ratchet forward the discovery of architectural character as a lead-up to the making of the solid building.

Immaculate detail compounds to carry on such a discussion in work such as Geraldine Booth's Nursery-Nursery project which was produced as a diploma project at the Bartlett School of Architecture, UCL, London, in 2006. It appears that both hand drawing and computer techniques have been combined to bring the Romanticism of the Pite-like world towards the sophistication of the 21st century. The whole thing is delightfully explicit: strangely it is able to be both quirky and tectonically controlled. It is a real 'architect's' drawing – with all the pedantic logging of rafters, tiles, frames and wraps, and then audacious things that happen to it all.

Thus it is in the tradition of drawings that simultaneously reassure the observer that they are competent and authentic – and then pile onto this a series of propositions that test the limitations of your comfortable culture.

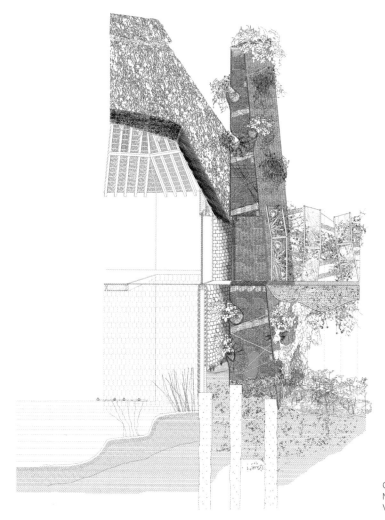

Geraldine Booth, Nursery-
Nursery, Browning's Island, Little
Venice, London, UK, 2006.

Such a test is even more clearly part of the agenda of the London-based
Portuguese-German architect Marcos Cruz.

The drawing featured here is part of his enormous Hyperdermis study (1999–
2001) that investigates skin, bulbous expansion of the skin to incorporate
chambers, and a to-and-fro inspiration from the territory of architecture and
the territory of organic and animal growth. Making experiments with latex
models and reading much about precedents (including the macabre and
the distasteful), Cruz moves in on his subject through a seemingly obsessive
compilation of quasi-organic cells. Richly varietous and in fairly spooky
territory, he expands upon the traditional method of plan drawing to feed in
three-dimensional bodies, body parts or body derivatives. His action is that of
delving, evacuating space rather that adding it.

In such a drawing there is, first of all, a demand on the spectator to stretch the mind outside the normal categories of 'flesh', 'built substance', 'membrane', 'apparatus', 'clothing' and the like. Yet the effect of a fairly consistent and almost sketchy technique with limited colour range is a (perhaps necessary) brake upon the danger of the proposition becoming too picturesque.

So we can now raise the issue of the curious relationship between exploration, sketch and formal assembly drawing (or any hybrid of all these), towards the act of creativity. Perhaps as a clue one might observe that in some architects' work the 'act' is more often a succession of stages of exploration: of a series of clarifications of intent. Just to add confusion to this analysis, however, we must respect the person who, having reached a state of clarification, sees the need to overlay another objective or criterion, and so the progress of the work is like a mist forming and clearing – and then forming again. The act of drawing, and particularly free-moving 'scribbled' drawing, enables this. Cruz is adept at this process and has a thorough grasp

Marcos Cruz, In-Wall Creatures, Plan 1:1 (Stage 2), Hyperdermis study, 1999–2001. Photoshop collage, ink drawing and photography.

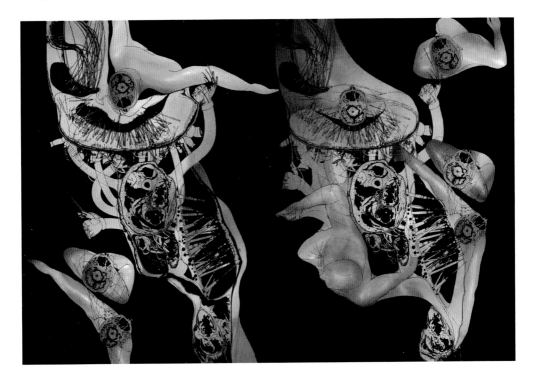

of scale and the likely scale of elements that are still not yet fully decided upon. This is an intriguing ability, evident in the work of many people in this book, and the observer has to take on trust any number of apparently functioning details, strange gizmos or unexplainable objects. Some of these might just be instinctual. Some of them might just be decoys. More often they will be germs of ideas that the creator wants to 'log' into the system via the drawing.

Thus the Hyperdermis drawing is a form of portmanteau – to be replaced or overlaid by later portmanteaux in which the status of its component parts is variable. That it nonetheless succeeds in giving us a strong 'feel' of the character of the idea is the result of Cruz's talent.

This same sense of 'delving' is very evident in the work of Nat Chard, the English architect who currently directs the School of Architecture at Winnipeg, Manitoba. Discussing two pairs of drawings enables us to see the role of successive sets of investigations that fuel a radical position in developing architecture. Moreover, much of Chard's work (as with some of Michael Webb's) is to do with optics, observation and controlled territories of vision.

Nat Chard, Layer 6: Third-Generation Architecture Built Within the Body, 2002. 5 x 4 Polaroid transfers and airbrush, stereoscopic pair.

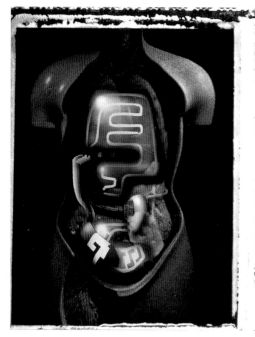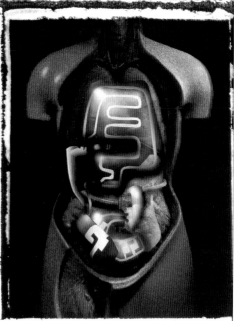

Nat Chard, Indeterminate
Apartment, Camden Town,
London, UK, 1999. 5 x 4
Polaroid transfers and airbrush,
stereoscopic pair.

Both Layer 6 (2002) and the Indeterminate Apartment (1999) are produced
as series of pairs of drawings. Readers with access to the lorgnette glasses
that read 3-D imagery will be able to get the full impact of these drawings.
But even without them, the proposition of the body project is to formalise
and then discuss analogies between the major functioning elements of the
human body and typical architectural or urbanistic arrangements.

The Indeterminate Apartment starts looking more like a piece of architecture
not least because the background elements are 'racks' or even conventional
built form to which the sculpted solid is an outrider. This outrider is not so very
different in form to some of the vessels held within the stomach in Layer 6, but
in the latter the shock of the context keeps them in separate parts of our mind.

Chard is sufficiently canny to overlay the fundamentals of these works with
decoy technique. Not for him a rough assemblage or a quick scribble, for
the ironies and the concentration upon detail must go together. Moreover,
the jumping out of flatness into three dimensions is very important to him.
His subsequent work on drawing machines and his work with students
involving 'prepared' cameras that enable you to draw onto the same film
that is taking the photograph, as well as his subsequent work in CAD/CAM

milling as drawing, are all related. The possibility of a continuous approach between 'controlled looking', the art of concentration and ways of drawing become, for him, a continuous sequence. Alongside this he has researched the American tradition of museum tableaux in which the impression of reality (usually for depicting animals in a landscape) is artificially created.

Remaining within the context of discussing drawings we are now nudging the territory of models, as we shall continue to do in the next chapter. The extension of the drawing tradition into computer modelling has achieved this transition almost seamlessly and it is not surprising that Chard moves backwards and forwards around this borderline. It is as if he is wishing to see more than he can see. Very much in the great tradition of architectural investigation. Da Vinci's sketches of machines leave us endlessly speculating about their foresightedness, Vladimir Tatlin is forgiven for designing an aeroplane that would never fly because it is more intriguing and more exploratory than many that do. All the time we must be ready to interrogate the architecture of the unlikely in order to push further the architecture of the predictable.

Drawings and 'near-drawings' have a special role in all this.

In-Built Metamorphosis

Over many years I have made series of drawings that take a proposition that predicts for itself a running, ever-changing metamorphosis. The 'Addhox Strip' (1970), the 'Urban Mark' (1971), the 'Trickling Towers' (1979), are some of these. The Veg House (1996-2001) brings together a number of secondary themes, such as the combination of natural growth with technical facilities, the manipulation of domestic space, the imperceptible barrier between house and garden, the delight of the vine, of the arbour, under the primary theme of 'Vegetation'.

For me, there is the delightful experience of carrying out a process that can enhance the primary decisions (of size, position, figure or direction), with such a mobile and extensive addition of evidence. It is as if the first part of the illustration is being illustrated by the second. Ingrained in my method is the base drawing. Major decisions are made. The relatively impermeable state of the base drawing is established (usually by making a print from the ink original). If a good watercolour paper is used, a considerable amount of trial and error is possible by laying down the watercolour and then sponging some

Peter Cook, Veg House, project metamorphosing over six stages: stages 1–4 1996, stages 5 and 6 2001. Plans and vignettes: line drawing and watercolour.

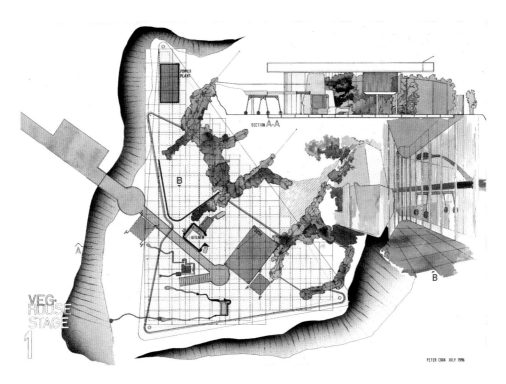

POWER PLANT

SECTION A-A

KITCHEN

B

Â

B̂

VEG·
HOUSE
STAGE
1

PETER COOK JULY 1996

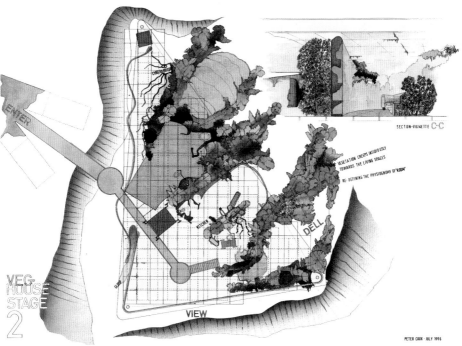

ENTER

CHILDREN

SECTION-VIGNETTE C-C

VEGETATION CREEPS INSIDIOUSLY
TOWARDS THE LIVING SPACES
RE-DEFINING THE PHYSIOGNOMY OF "ROOM"

KITCHEN

DELL

GLIDE

VIEW

VEG·
HOUSE
STAGE
2

PETER COOK · JULY 1996

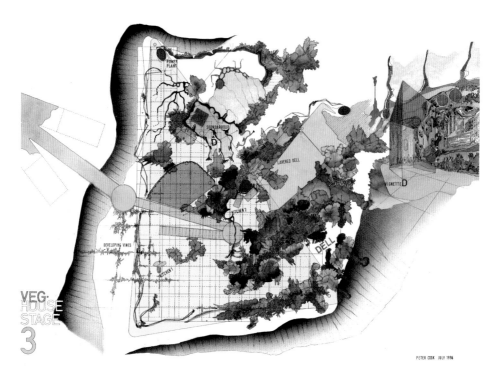

VEG-
HOUSE
STAGE
3

PETER COOK JULY 1996

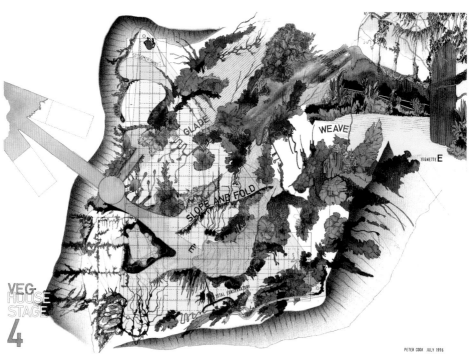

VEG-
HOUSE
STAGE
4

PETER COOK JULY 1996

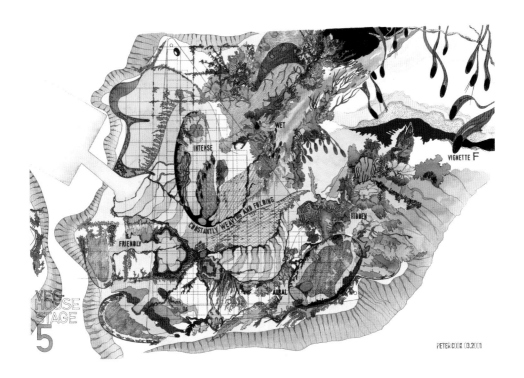

VEG HOUSE STAGE 5

INTENSE

WET

VIGNETTE F

CONSTANTLY WEARING AND FOLDING

FRIENDLY

HIDDEN

AURAL

PETER COOK 03.2001

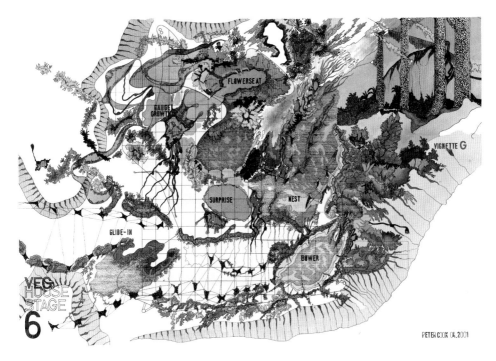

VEG HOUSE STAGE 6

FLOWERSEAT

GAUGE GROWTH

VIGNETTE G

SURPRISE

NEST

GLIDE-IN

BOWER

PETER COOK 04.2001

of it out and replacing it with an alternative series of colours. More drawing can be added on top and there is also, of course, the possibility of coloured pencils or patches of inkwork to be added.

In fact, the Veg House proceeded without much deviation. The convention of a plan drawing, amplified by a vignette drawing on the top right-hand corner, was enough to carry the six stages of metamorphosis of the house from a relatively circumspect layout of bed area, living area and suchlike through to a wild, wayward and deliberately hybridised series of conditions that flow and melt into each other.

One can track the stages of the gradual breakdown of 'order' that leads to a (presumed) magical new order. The ability of watercolour to relate the controlled vegetation to the hybrid and to change – by colour and intensity – the mode of enclosure cannot be overstated. It is an ideal medium for defining and then softening. Ideal for initially being familiar, in colour or texture, and then rather more exotic in the same terms. Creatively the project expressed a series of general intentions that were only looking one or two stages ahead: deliberately following the implications of an accumulated thrust. Almost suggesting the next move by themselves.

The increasing use of key descriptive or suggestive words as part of the drawing itself, such as 'dell', 'arbour' or 'flow', recalls the much earlier period of Archigram and serves both as a reference for the spectator and something of an incentive for the designer.

Add to this the attempt to capture the phenomenon of plantation as a component of organised space: always about to grow out of control and grow towards some unpredictable formation. Add to this the wish to predict apparatus and inventions about which one can be no more than instinctive, such as the combination of kitchen appliances and bushes, relaxing furniture and foliage, tree growth and electrical circuitry – and you weave yourself into a Romantic area of pictorialisation.

In this chapter, we have moved into detail but have hardly become less heroic in the process. The exploration of architecture runs way beyond the search for icons or grand plans, and perhaps in looking at the localised surfaces and contrivances we can reflect the minutiae of our own experiences as a mirror of the architecture itself.

Beyond Drawing– Beyond Reality 9

Bit by bit, I have found myself edging this collection and my commentary towards a point where an admission has to be made: that architectural drawings are easily able to transcend any reference to reality. Yet this is not some abstract or nihilistic position; more an ambition that is essentially borne of the belief that architecture has much left to discover and that the architect can make drawings that transport him or her into a form of séance. Such a state is arguably necessary if we are not to constantly project bits and pieces of ideas that are constantly referred back (and implicitly held back) by any insistence upon the necessary, with justification of the circumspect, an implicit Puritanism of the ordinary or simply the necessity to always quote from the realisable. This last relationship between an architectural drawing and the buildable has already been touched upon. At this stage, however, I wish to open up the most heady and scary prospect of all, which is to discuss work which can only partly be verified, or which treads completely into the unknown. Only some of which actually looks like architecture.

The history of the recent past vehemently suggests that we should be less timid than we often are in acknowledging the role of things that look like nothing we have ever seen before – indeed there are so many components of the electronic world that are virtually invisible (as well as the impulses they generate which are, of course, totally invisible). There are all those mechanical complexes and electronic-electrical-mechanical combinations in which the chain of events becomes unfathomable to the non-specialist.

What a distance it is that has been run from the moral imperative of recognisable rightness, of the idea of a functional aesthetic, or the 'fitness for purpose' morality as a set of visible mannerisms. Every time we fly we are at the mercy of unseen electronics, and if the bits and pieces that we can see look purposeful enough we are aware that they too are the handmaidens of those mysterious silicon chips and circuitry.

Yet we refuse to lose faith in the tradition of 'stuff' and 'things'. Along with the revival of interest in 'the diagram' is the notion that a 'path of action' or the 'strategy' surrounding a phenomenon can add up to a tangible aesthetic. We are becoming increasingly familiar with the apparently absurd and the intangible really taking place in every field, and we may soon have a collective tolerance that will manifest itself in a mass taste for the weird and the unexpected as such and the obscure might merge with the vernacular.

Many architects might resist this even if the general public will have a ready taste for it, and there is some historical evidence to suggest that the architectural avant-garde or the professional leadership lurches in one direction or the other vis-à-vis popular taste: running towards the classical or Rational in periods of exuberant culture, or running wild in periods of economic or moral restraint. Add to this the lateral spread of ideas across territory: remember the taste for chinoiserie among the 19th-century Europeans, the taste for Americana among aspirant societies in the mid-20th century or the cyclical push-pull of Regionalism or Internationalism?

It is even conceivable that there will be a period of creativity around a kind of faux reality. If architecture no longer needs to depict or even reflect real functional parts (because these are virtually invisible), then the discipline might escape into a form of 'theatre' whereby a satisfyingly elegant or complicated set of visible things is made available, almost none of which have any operational meaning: but they're fun anyhow. Consider a situation where nearly all architecture is a folly?

In positing such a world I am neither encouraging it nor holding off in expectation. More, I am clearing the ground for the presentation of this final batch of drawings, suggesting that they are, in fact, quite wholesome and steadily continuing in the tradition of invention and the documentation of ideas.

A Field of Speculation

If, therefore, The Undifferentiated Fluid (1998) by Graeme Williamson of London-based Block Architecture is not immediately recognisable as architecture (though it is in fact an illustration of a constructible, woven surface), it somewhat reassures us because of its connotations with vegetable growth. Disturbing in its trails of beaded light. Reassuring again in its array of pod-like tubes. Disturbing in the sinister implication of an unlikely colour for a natural growth. Reassuring again with its laced thongs.

In describing it thus – alternately by a challenge and then a reassurance – I am perhaps parodying the far more spontaneous dissection that we undertake when we glance at contemporary architectural imagery resting the unknown upon the known (or presumed) and clinging onto the hope that it all adds up. Too few innovatory drawers attempt to spell out the significance of the parts in words. Even fewer dare to expose a theory or logic. It is assumed that there is a form of Expressionism involved – or occasionally the claim of a technical demonstration of some sort. Moreover, in this case it is mostly hand-painted and thus there is the intrigue in it as a piece of technique.

In the case of Michael Webb's drawings for the Temple Island project (1988), illustrated in Chapter 2, the delight in the drawn and painted technique acts as both a decoy away from the intriguing nature of the proposition and as a celebration of the inherent magic of (and in his case, nostalgia for) its site.

Webb's technique has often adapted and developed in order to heighten the apparent reality of a surface, which acts brilliantly to point out the originality of the actual propositions. For the last 20 years, Temple Island has acted as a field for speculation and discussion among architects and academics. So we can readily speculate upon the power that the drawing in itself adds to its intellectual fascination.

At the other extreme, I can comment very specifically about a drawing that summarises a certain magic but equally contains matter-of-fact information. Effectively a diagram, the BIX facade (2003) by Toronto-based artist/ programmer Jeremy Rotsztain in collaboration with realities:united of Berlin, enables the Kunsthaus in Graz that Colin Fournier and myself designed to become a pixelated and illuminated facade. The drawing is absolutely key to the experience of the building and carries with it a direct representation

Graeme Williamson, The
Undifferentiated Fluid (partial
object), 1998. Palette knife
through oil-based printing ink
on vellum.

of the fluorescent rings that straddle the surface: yet it is also a form of
'instruction' drawing. The wiring layout is at the core of the game, yet it has
something a little less abstract about it than those drawings that one finds in
hi-fi booklets. For one thing, it records the oblique geometry as the surface
turns away from you: so it is a 'picture' while still logging each and every
interface condition.

One is reminded of the relationship between the musical score and the
experience of the music itself. If we follow this association we can predict
a developing taste for such diagrams. After all, there was a brief period in
which art galleries toyed with the selling of architects' technical drawings,
and there is already (since their demise) a nostalgia for those white lines
on blue background known as 'blueprints'. It serves to satisfy the quest for
'authenticity' if nothing else.

realities:united architects,
BIX Communicative Display
Skin for the Kunsthaus Graz,
Austria, 2003.

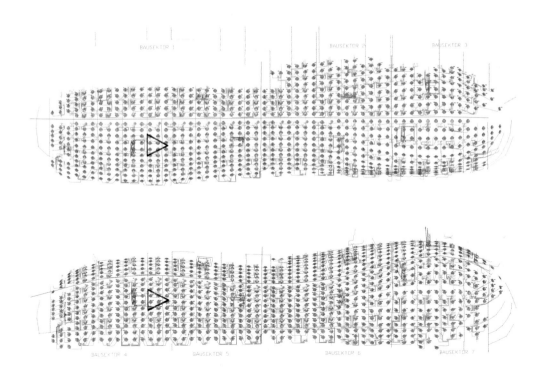

Holding Off the Tedium of Reality

The distillation of an architectural dream can sometimes be made through a very carefully chosen language of simplified or coded forms. Neither exactly abstract nor exactly figurative. Such are the drawings of Madelon Vriesendorp that were made in the early days – many of them to articulate the architectural statements of her husband, Rem Koolhaas. Her painting for the Welfare Palace Hotel project (1976) on Roosevelt Island in New York City

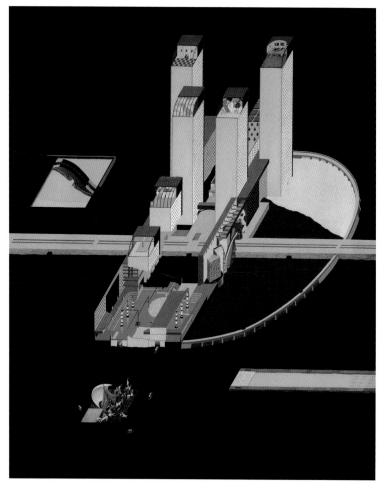

Rem Koolhaas, Welfare Palace Hotel, Roosevelt Island, New York, US, 1976. Cutaway axonometric: gouache on paper, 129.5 x 102.9 cm. Painting by Madelon Vriesendorp.

has an aesthetic of simple planes and blocks, topped and articulated by small areas of tasty detail. Almost like confectionery, it tickles the palette without having to give too much away about the arrangements within. It is both a symbol of an architecture and a delightful artefact. Yet somehow it holds off, away from the tedium of reality. It suggests heroism, it suggests 'specialness' – and this was surely part of the agenda for the Office of Metropolitan Architecture. The blackness of the ground (or is it not water?) assists such an otherworldliness. The quality of 'play' is held by the power of it as a flat graphic: an art that is now constantly under threat from the tendency towards photographic reality – easily possible in computer renderings.

Mystery and temptation are held by an 'unreal' that nonetheless has a reference back to the 'real' but refuses to ape it.

However, we can move one degree further towards the real and still maintain a useful distance. Is it not debatable whether the people that would have commissioned the venerable master of architectural presentation Helmut Jacoby in the mid- to late 20th century were merely seeking a reliable, predictable and technically brilliant rendition – and would have rushed towards the computer-based techniques had they been available. By doing so they might have missed the subtle quality of prioritisation that Jacoby gives us in his drawing for the (then) new town of Milton Keynes.

Helmut Jacoby, Town Park, Water Carpet and Cone Area, Milton Keynes, UK, 1976.

In his depiction of the Town Park, Water Carpet and Cone Area (1976) he recalls something of the 18th-century grand, tailored, 'open' countryside that

is at the core of English landscape planning. The drawing, in its fine-grain monochromy, maintains memories of this atmosphere, as often depicted in etchings and contemporary prints. It is an idyllic, if controlled, world. Finely balanced, but never actually realised. The tectonic essentials are pulled a little more into focus than they would be in a photograph. The natural growth is a little more controlled than it could be in fact. So here again the discrimination is there at the hands of the person making the drawing, and the flawless technique leaves us in no doubt about the designed intention as well as its social intention.

We can already view such a culture with some cynicism since technique, politics and taste are conveniently linked in the work. Clearly there are cyclic modes whereby this linkage becomes closer and further apart. The etching spanned a very considerable period of architectural metamorphosis but seemed to handle the detail of both Classicism and Gothic, and the concoctions that emanated from both. Pencil and watercolour were best with ambiguity. The ink line could scamper between the technical instruction and a range of departures from such instruction. Combinatory techniques – ink and wash, photographic collage and drawing, mechanical tone and hand drawing – all tend to deter the faint-hearted but are eminently capable. One welcomes a moment when the adherents of both hand drawing and computer rendering start to join forces on the same sheet of paper. It is starting to happen and surely mirrors the reality of architecture itself as the inevitable product of both the world of 'hands off' production and rough, tough and dirty site work.

A full detachment from all this and the enjoyment of a dreamy, magical world was surely expressed by a now forgotten student in the class of AA Vesnin at VKhUTEMAS, the Russian state art and technical school, founded in 1920 in Moscow. Produced at the height of the period when both that teacher and many colleagues were creating their heroic pieces of Constructivist Soviet architecture, what is extraordinary about Nikolai Sokolov's drawing of a Health-Resort Hotel (1928) is its winsome quality: a direct mannerism, a sweetness that owes nothing to the toughness or mechanical nature of Constructivist buildings and little to their sheer walls and dramatic contraptions. Indeed, the predominant characteristic of this work is its constrained flowerbed of detached pieces. Almost wallpaper-like in their purity and disposition, the buildings themselves are little chambers supporting these parasols (or are they fruits?) in the pursuit of a healthy retreat. Yet at that time few, if any, models of such a place could have existed.

Nikolai Sokolov, Health-Resort Hotel (VKhUTEMAS, studio of AA Vesnin), Moscow, Russia, 1928. Axonometric: ink, watercolour, gouache and white ink on paper, 108.5 x 36.2 cm.

At once we are in a parallel territory to that of the Welfare Palace Hotel, where the lack of detail preserves the freshness of the proposition. There is just a minimum delineation of an opened door, a flimsy bridge and some horizontal balustrading. In some respects it fails to be a competent drawing in the Helmut Jacoby sense, and it stops far short of being a diagram: yet it is those limitations that seem to add charm to the thing and question, once again, our dependence upon normal criteria of quality when dealing with drawn architecture.

The Exploratory Scribble as Model

Withdrawing from the conventional perfection still further leads us naturally in a full circle towards the 'idea-scribble'. Again it is Wolf Prix of Viennese practice Coop Himmelb(l)au, featured in Chapter 1, who can engage us. Unlike the house-scribble on page 18, he is here proposing a contraption, the 'Dosen-wolke' for a gallery in Düsseldorf, that is part dream, part gadget, part inflatable, part mechanism and perhaps part art-piece and part architecture.

Coop Himmelb(l)au, Dosen-Wolke 1968. Collage (photo and sketch) on paper.

What must have seemed, at the time, a highly radical assemblage of provocative elements – spheres, tubes, cylinders and a composition that was probably quite unnerving to the Viennese bourgeoisie – does not seem to need the rhetoric of the wild drawing, though Prix and Swiczinsky of Himmelb(l)au are able to pursue here a grouping of parts that they had hitherto only combined in small installations. Indeed, the drawn part of the collage is almost deceptively calm: lulling us into believing the utter *reasonableness* of the proposition while stating its ambition by the very *architecturalness* of its scale. So here we have drawing used as information and (possibly) at the same time as palliative.

More than 30 years later Prix (and by now a heavyweight studio) is still producing dynamic and wayward gyrations. It seemed necessary to break the rules in a book about drawing to inscribe a piece that is, technically, a model, but to all intents and purposes is an exploratory scribble of the same feverish intent as the Düsseldorf exhibit. It examines the first ideas for the ZAK – Zukunftsakademie in Haslau, Austria (1999) and sets a handful of enclosures of incomplete organicism up into space. It dangles, or more likely casts – in the way of a fishing line – a series of tracks, in much the same way as the scribbles and dotted lines of the earlier piece. Since it is a physical object, and made quickly, it does not worry about convention: the vertical poles are merely necessary so that the plexiglas trays are there somewhere to locate the really important (and irregular) elements.

Such a piece comes out of the drawing tradition – or even its cousin, the collage tradition. It is spatial, but in this case only secondarily so. It sets up a series of almost floating parts that can congeal or take off at a later stage. In a way it points to one vexed issue that besets the truly exploratory designer when making a drawing: namely the state of response when you have made the marks. Even if the intention (or logic) is that the scheme will develop and metamorphose in terms of the positions of the parts or the mannerisms involved, you have the thing there and it may satisfy. It may look agreeable as a picture. Yet it must conceptually and dynamically move on.

The model, by contrast – however agreeable – has the tempting and irritating habit of inviting you to look at the parts from a variety of viewpoints. Some good and some less so. It may have the capability to be reconfigured in a matter of seconds. Yet against this is the tiresome fact that fashioning a physical model, even a simple one, takes more time than the deft sketch. Computer animations or even straightforward computer-drawn constructs

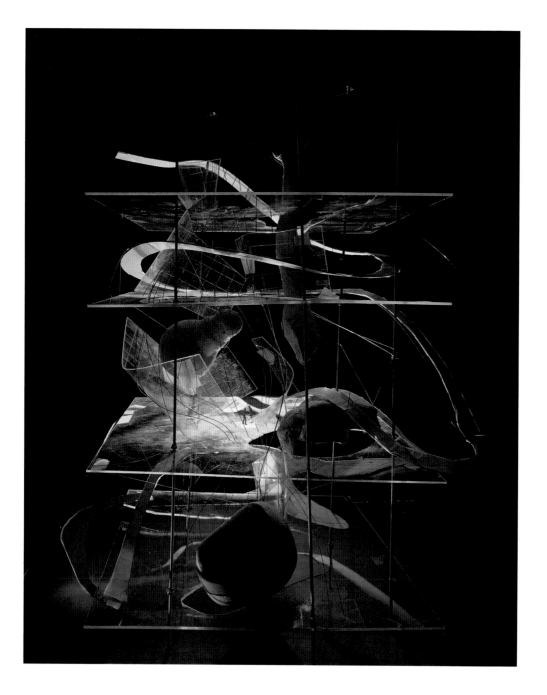

Coop Himmelb(l)au, ZAK
– Zukunftsakademie, Haslau,
Austria, 1999.

have a certain disciplinary stiffness, demanding a logic for the displacement of parts. So the complex continues. This is why this particular model is interesting in its willingness to retain an ambiguity towards position, solidity, figurative consistency, plus the temptation of those dangling wisps and what they might suggest for the next stage of the composition.

West Coast Wonderland

In the hands of a master designer and manipulator of digitalised exploration, the same investigations that we have seen with the Prix work can be the core of apparently 'formed' compositions. In a series of 2002 drawings, the original cyberspace pioneer, the Venezuelan-born, West-Coast based Marcos Novak suggests an arrangement of claws or blades and interstitial spaces that will hardly remain in that configuration for more than a second. Or at least that is an implication that can be made at two levels: they can move, as do a bird's feathers or an aeroplane's fins. At the other level, this particular 'frozen' moment is that of the investigation itself. Rearrangement can involve the substitution of new major elements for old. Furthermore, the substitution or

Marcos Novak, AlloBio, 2002.

rearrangement can be part of the modification of strategy. With moments of realisation and exploratory discovery emerging all the time.

Thus the potential of rapid reconfiguration that would have been a mammoth task – becoming a bore – in traditional hand drawing, is bypassed by the ability of the computer to make such moves. The necessity, with all these methods, is to keep open the creative trajectory. Novak has made many explorations of inhabiting virtual space, demonstrating in experiments and exhibitions the possibility of affecting space without the placement of conventional solid objects. Some of these have no drawn record and therefore come outside the scope of this book.

Yet it seems necessary to re-examine the tradition of drawing as related to design intention and keep it in mind as a living conceptual force.

The delight and charm of Novak's contraptions as such is therefore to be measured against such a criterion. As with Michael Webb's Temple Island (see Chapter 2), the two directions of the seduction work well together.

Also working from the Los Angeles area, Hernán Díaz Alonso seems at first to seduce us with almost excessive visual guile (see also Alonso's PS1 MoMA Pavilion in Chapter 4). Somehow the creative ambience of southern California seems to breed from the inherited atmosphere of wonderland, though the real reason may be more to do with the very admixture of aerospace and car design, film-making, graphic and advertising incentives, and advanced education that revolves around Cal-Tech, Cal-Arts and UCLA. SCI-ARC and the mysterious sheds in Burbank or Culver City where numerous commercial outfits extend the languages of graphics and form.

Alonso's sculptural installation Sangre (Spanish for 'blood'), created for a monographic exhibition at the San Francisco Museum of Modern Art in 2006, comes from an architectural mind that has found itself located within a special culture of digitalised exploration and response. Yet compared with many of his contemporaries, Alonso is definitely a romantic and visionary who developed his language of space and elements as a disciple of Enric Miralles – who only briefly engaged with the computer. Another key influence, and fellow inhabitant of Los Angeles, is Greg Lynn. Although still a young man, Lynn is already seen as a Godfather figure in the digital world. His own pursuit of parametric modelling and its integration with art-based surfaces develops continuously. Alonso, however, is aesthetically more daring and

Hernán Díaz Alonso, Sangre, Design Series IV, San Francisco Museum of Modern Art, 2006. Animation-based software, 1024 x 768 pixels.

has a feel for occurrent space – a characteristic that positively indulges in the minutiae of form and the potential of a total design to enjoy the differences between one element, part, zone, gadget or whatever we might describe as the reason for differentiation. Thus his work is rarely satisfied with a mere rolling surface or a single set of relationships, characteristics that are criticisable from outside the coteries of parametric design adherents.

His verve and an enthusiastic personality fit exactly to the parallel charisma of his designs. Sangre has an otherworldly character and sits well as a connotation between located parts (the translucent domes) and implications of liquidity (the flowing, red treacle between). If an earlier generation has delighted in the role to be played by mechanics in the realisation of metamorphic architecture, then his can delight in the potential for softer and even more fundamental metamorphosis: the possibilities of nanotechnology and the 'growing' of tectonic flesh and surfaces, for instance.

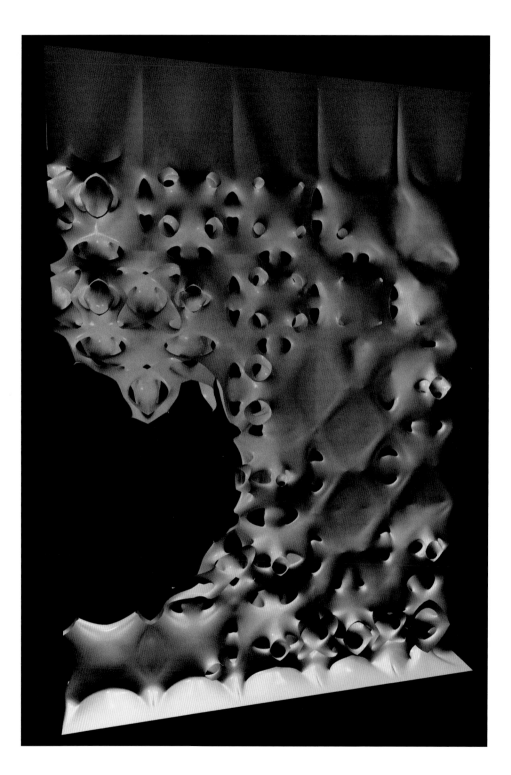

Creativity Explored

New York-based Sulan Kolatan and William MacDonald extend their range and begin to convince us that the implication of real substance can be brought so far forward that we are almost convinced that the object is real. As the processes or programmes move forward, and since this clutch of architects are so visually sensitive, we become reassured that the value of the work lies in its creativity and the 'reality' of it has its own value as a piece of architectural politics. Such is the rhetoric of the real.

The edges of drawing explode again through the more recent work of Lebbeus Woods. That someone with such complete technique is not satisfied to just roll it out and satisfy his wide public with more of the same is clear to audiences at his memorable lectures. Genuinely a thinker and an explorer, asking many questions of the social and political conditions of cities and mastering space from an analytical assessment of structure and process, Woods continues to be restless.

Not least in his Vienna explorations of 2005, where a number of jottings of the actual physicality of a Vienna street are overlaid by energy lines based upon his reading of the city as a force field, and then realised as an actual installation.

Look closely at the illustration and you will discover evidence of the existence of light fittings and shadows. Yet it is at the same time a figure in a series with the other drawings. In certain respects we have jumped just as we did in the Wolf Prix Coop Himmelb(l)au model. All the instincts and hierarchies of the piece are of a drawing: with the thicker, red shards seen against the dashes of white shards which are then challenged by the more evocative weaving of the thicker white rods. At some point the play of light and the role played by the floor can be said to interfere – or lie in a further territory of interplay – with the set-up so far.

Sulan Kolatan and William MacDonald (KOL/MAC LLC), INVERSAbrane high-performance ecological exterior/interior building membrane system, 2005. Digitally rendered image file (using Autodesk Maya software).

All the time in contemplating this piece we are passing backwards and forwards between flat compositions with some spatial and categorisatory values, or alternatively a space with graphic and linear values per se. So as Woods' work both here and in chapter 6 becomes more abstract than illustrative, it becomes more generically spatial.

This once again suggests that there is no real gap between drawing and modelling. Standing within the piece, there was no ambiguity to be felt,

Lebbeus Woods, System Wien,
Energy buildings #1 and #3,
2005. Ink on paper.

since wherever you stood and turned, from every direction there was the experience of a 'drawing' – through the clarity and definition of the lines and then, on turning, another, related drawing.

The Drawing Redefined

Moving finally to the techniques now available to us through the ability of the computer to be linked to the modelling machine, we have moved right into a condition that seems to have obviated the very need for making drawings. The manoeuvres of the controlled mouse span from the hand straight through to a solid, fashioned object. It is not our role here to describe the technology involved, but to examine just how much this activity carries on the role of stating an aim and working it through in a single run of moves. If we can prove that it does – and the evidence from aficionados of the pursuit suggests that this is so – then we have a creative relationship between the designer and the artefact that is intriguingly similar to that of making the drawing. If we allow that the need for a drawing to be specifically on paper, or on a flat surface, made with lines or with patches of identifiable territory, presenting an identifiable image or pattern, is too limited, and if we allow that it can span a wider range of visual territory (of course created through a range of media impulses), then we can admit as a 'drawing' a figuration like that of Tobias Klein's facade of the Chapel of Our Lady de Regla for Havana. Submitted as his final-year project at the Bartlett in 2006 (and as a student of Colletti and Cruz) his work derives its design from religious relics and three-dimensional scans of animal bones.

Having admitted that Woods' Vienna exhibit is still, creatively, a drawing, we only have to go a couple of steps further to admit the same about this piece. Moreover, Klein approached the design as a worked arrangement of related patterns and elements. So far the piece remains relatively shallow, but not absolutely flat. The tradition of bas-relief is not exactly at stake here, even if that might open up a further angle on this question of 'what is the definition of a drawing?' Such a work reminds us that a whole generation of designers is now lining up to jump beyond the traditional and defined boundary. Purists and nostalgics will be afraid of the loss of the drawing tradition, yet they need have no fear. Watching the way in which Klein and his friends manipulate the medium and talking to them about their motives and motions, one is immediately reassured – even reminded – of the old drawing-as-design procedures.

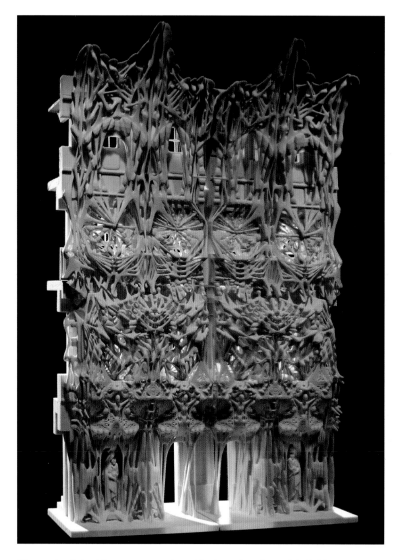

Tobias Klein, facade of the altar space in the inverted chapel of Our Lady de Regla, Havana, Cuba, Synthetic Syncretism project, 2006. Model: additive process, rapid manufactured using Z-Corp technology.

Circumstantial evidence came to be critical as when I met Mark West, a Professor at the University of Manitoba. He is most widely known as the Director of the Centre for Architectural Structures and Technology (CAST), which develops alternative construction and design methods, including the use of flexible fabric formwork for the production of reinforced-concrete structures. His dedicated research laboratory is a large studio where he and his colleagues make a variety of objects: ordered, free or admixtures of all definitions of form. These have pushed forward our ideas about concrete as a component and certainly pushed out the limits of sculpted prefabrication and the like. Enjoying this I was then recommended by Nat Chard – Head of the Department of Architecture at the university – to see West's collection of

Mark West, Welcome To The Neighbourhood, 1985. Graphite on paper photocollage, 32 x 35 cm.

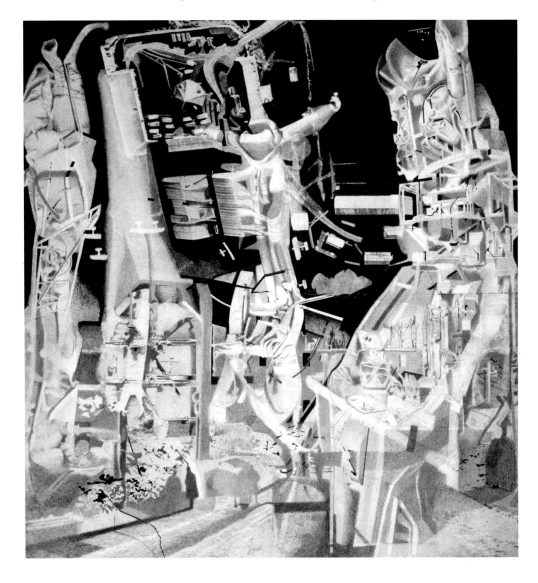

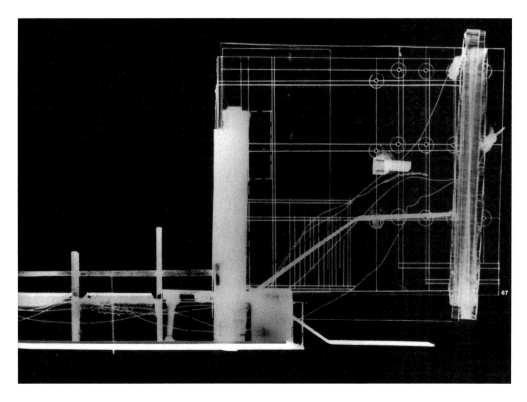

drawings. They go to extraordinary lengths of depiction. They are completely original. They are consistently produced by pencil: whereby they incorporate both the normal, additive process of such work, but can also proceed by covering the paper surface with graphite and then working backwards through the use of an eraser, so that the white spaces are 'carved' out of the black space.

West worked as a building contractor during and before his student days at the School of Architecture at Cooper Union in New York. Admitting to the influence of both John Hejduk and Sverre Fehn as his teachers, and hitherto having had a few exhibitions, he is certainly a creative, visionary architect. It is difficult, too, to suggest a better or more manipulable medium for the purpose.

It is as if the threat of the camera has been left behind a long time ago, despite the ironic fact that many of the computer-generated sequences and juxtapositions stem from investigations that started through photographic manipulation. The pushing, pulling, melting, sleight of hand and the emergence of a truly mixed medium paralleled the search for a visual world at the edge of reality. The passing of light onto sensitive paper – a technique invented by Man Ray, beloved of the Surrealists and others of the European avant-garde of the 1930s – has been appropriated by young architects such as Simon Haycock. Once again, it can be defined as 'drawing' because of its procedure of placement and discrimination. The result is mainly linear, but with an atmospheric overtone. To what extent this overtone is creative or merely depictive is an issue. The effect of the argument is to make us ponder upon the degree to which a certain 'buzz' comes from the delight of the gently hinted at, as opposed to the 'in your face' line drawing. This, the 'ray-o-gram', has the air of a byway in the broad stream of architectural depiction, perhaps bypassed by both the voracity of the computer and the convenience of the hand drawing.

A 'teaser' that I cannot resist as we reach the final stage of the discussion is an inventive piece by the German architect-academic Nikolaus Parmasche. His student project for a series of buildings that are floating on the River Main, at Frankfurt would be remarkable enough since it elegantly posits the idea of a building that 'hinges' itself off the river bank. It can reconfigure and, indeed, despite its graphic quality, so can the piece illustrated here. For it is a model. Photographed flat on and with a certain linearity it almost reads as a drawing. Again, it causes one to ponder on the issue of the boundaries of architectural drawing.

Nikolaus Parmasche, Floating and Shifting Buildings, River Main Frankfurt, Germany, 1990. Cardboard model and pencil on photograph.

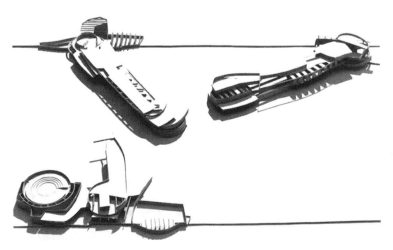

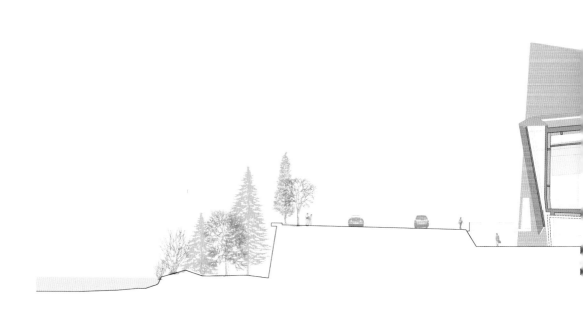

Yet in all this I have been writing as a designer: with my own primary motive of making drawings for the purposes of making buildings – or at least building ideas. Needing to push the conceptual range further and further on and needing to constantly complete the cycle between ideas and forms, forms and arrangements, arrangements and motives, motives and content, content and ideas.

Peter Cook, Gavin Robotham Salvador Pérez Arroyo: Crab Studio, Verbania Municipal Theatre, Italy, 2007. Section: computer-generated drawing.

It is useful to reflect on this whole business of drawing through the reflective lens of the building process itself. As someone known for so long as a paper architect who now builds, I sometimes wonder whether the special moment of realisation of an idea exists at the 'drawn' end of the process or at the handing-over date for the finished object. As I implied in Chapter 7, the drawings of the Kunsthaus in Graz (a building that has brought my friend Colin Fournier and I a certain tangible notoriety) give the lie to both moments. A building of this size is a complex machine and there is a constant process of 'tuning' involved.

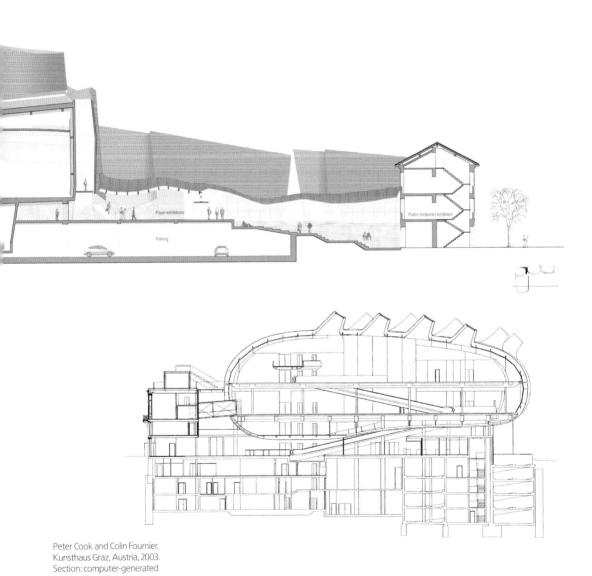

Peter Cook and Colin Fournier,
Kunsthaus Graz, Austria, 2003.
Section: computer-generated
line drawing.

If the building was 95 per cent consistent in ideas, through from the competition stage to completion, there is one drawing – and it is the section – that summarises both the total lyricism and the necessary constituency of parts.

Sections are out of fashion at the moment, but due for a revival. That most delightful of drawing types, they are able to offer both 'picture' and 'organisation'. After all, a plan serves to deal with organisation and an elevation gives a picture. Both of these can be total – as far as they go. Various types of three-dimensional drawing can give a picture, but however evocative, it is a biased – a directional – view. The section is the aficionado's choice. Buildings can be infinitely debated through the forensic analysis of a section. The virtuoso manipulator will recognise in another's section his wit and her architectural literacy.

The section is perhaps the most irritating and intangible form of architects' drawing for the untrained eye. It confounds those critics who try to ascribe a value system that is not based upon form and operation (a larger contingent than is strictly necessary). It is a joy. The long section of the Kunsthaus Graz says it all. It is both technical and conceptual.

Right up to the moment of completing this book, one is still predominantly designing through the section for the Municipal Theatre at Verbania on Italy's Lake Maggiore – a building that must absorb the subtleties of 'localness' and the social life of both day-to-day events, as well as the 'theatre' that exists before and after the performance proper. So – almost as I write – my colleagues at the Crab Studio and I push and pull, hone and tweak the profiles: as you only can do in section.

Index